The Palladium of Justice

BOOKS BY LEONARD W. LEVY

The Law of the Commonwealth and Chief Justice Shaw
Legacy of Suppression: Freedom of Speech and Press in Early American History
The American Political Process, editor
Jefferson and Civil Liberties: The Darker Side
Major Crises in American History: Documentary Problems, editor
Congress, editor
The Judiciary, editor
Political Parties and Pressure Groups, editor
The Presidency, editor
American Constitutional Law: Historical Essays
Freedom of the Press from Zenger to Jefferson
Freedom and Reform, editor
Origins of the Fifth Amendment: The Right Against Self-Incrimination
Essays on the Making of the Constitution, editor
The Fourteenth Amendment and the Bill of Rights, editor
Judgments: Essays on American Constitutional History
The Supreme Court Under Warren, editor
Blasphemy in Massachusetts, editor
Treason Against God: A History of the Offense of Blasphemy
Emergence of a Free Press
Constitutional Opinions: Aspects of the Bill of Rights
The Establishment Clause: Religion and the First Amendment
Encyclopedia of the American Constitution, editor
The Framing and Ratification of the Constitution, editor
The American Founding, editor
Original Intent and the Framers' Constitution
Encyclopedia of the American Constitution, Supplement One, editor
Blasphemy: Verbal Offense Against the Sacred from Moses to Salman Rushdie
Encyclopedia of the American Presidency, editor
Seasoned Judgments: Constitutional Rights and American History
A License to Steal: The Forfeiture of Property
Origins of the Bill of Rights

The PALLADIUM
of JUSTICE

Origins of Trial by Jury

Leonard W. Levy

IVAN R. DEE

CHICAGO 1999

Library of Congress Cataloging-in-Publication Data:
Levy, Leonard Williams, 1923–
    The palladium of justice : origins of trial by jury / Leonard W. Levy.
      p. cm.
    Includes bibliographical references and index.
    ISBN 1-56663-259-5 (acid-free paper)
    1. Jury—Great Britain—History. 2. Jury—United States—History.
I. Title
KD7540.L48 1999
345.42'075—dc21
                                    99-12923

To Wendy Ellen and Leslie Anne

My daughters for whom I care greatly

but who care little about my books

CONTENTS

The Palladium of Justice

CHAPTER I

❧

Rival Systems of Criminal Justice

TRIAL BY JURY is the mainstay of the accusatorial system of criminal justice. Accusatorial procedure antedated the Norman Conquest. From the early Middle Ages, civil and ecclesiastical authorities throughout western Europe had employed substantially similar accusatorial procedures. The latter half of the twelfth century and the first half of the thirteenth was a period of transition that witnessed profound transformations of procedure. Old forms of trial, once universal, broke down and newer ones emerged. In England the new forms, presentment (the formal statement of an offense, presented to authority) and trial by jury, preserved the accusatorial character of the old; on the Continent and in the ecclesiastical courts, inquisitorial procedure was triumphant. By no coincidence, the liberties of the subject were to thrive in England and be throttled on the Continent.

Community courts and community justice prevailed in

England at the time of the Norman Conquest. The legal system was ritualistic, dependent upon oaths at most stages of litigation, and permeated by both religious and superstitious
notions. Legal concepts were so primitive that no distinction
existed between civil and criminal cases or between secular and
ecclesiastical cases. Proceedings were oral, very personal, and
highly confrontative. Juries were unknown. One party publicly
"appealed," or accused, the other in front of a community
meeting at which the presence of both was obligatory. Absence
meant risking fines and outlawry. After the preliminary statements of the parties, the court rendered judgment, not on the
merits of the issue or the question of guilt or innocence, but on
the manner by which it should be resolved. Judgment, in other
words, preceded trial, because it was a decision on what form
the trial should take. It might be by compurgation, by ordeal,
or, after the Norman Conquest, by battle. Excepting trial by
battle, only one party was tried or, more accurately, was put to
his "proof." Proof being regarded as an advantage, it was usually awarded to the accused party; in effect, he had the privilege of proving his own case.

Trial by exculpatory oath and compurgation, also called
canonical purgation, consisted of a sworn statement to the truth
of one's claim or denial, supported by the oaths of a certain
number of fellow swearers. Presumably they would not endan-
ger their immortal souls by the sacrilege of false swearing.
Originally the oath-helpers swore from their own knowledge
to the truth of the party's claim. Later they became little more
than character witnesses, swearing only to their belief that his
oath was trustworthy. If he rounded up the requisite number

of compurgators and the cumbrous swearing in very exact form proceeded without a mistake, he won his case. A mistake "burst" the oath, proving guilt.

Ordeals were usually reserved for more serious crimes, for persons of bad reputation, for peasants, or for those caught with stolen goods. As an invocation of immediate divine judgment, ordeals were consecrated by the church and shrouded with solemn religious mystery. The accused underwent a physical trial in which he called upon God to witness his innocence by putting a miraculous sign upon his body. Cold water, boiling water, and hot iron were the principal ordeals, all of which the clergy administered. In the ordeal of cold water, the accused was trussed up and cast into a pool to see whether he would sink or float. On the theory that water which had been sanctified by a priest would receive an innocent person but reject the guilty, innocence was proved by sinking—and with luck a quick retrieval; guilt was proved by floating. In the other ordeals, one had to plunge his hand into a cauldron of boiling water or carry a red-hot piece of iron for a certain distance, in the hope that three days later, when the bandages were removed, a priest would find a "clean" wound, one that was healing free of infection. How deeply one plunged his arm into the water, how heavy the iron or great the distance it was carried, depended mainly on the gravity of the charge.

The Normans brought to England still another ordeal, trial by battle, paradigm of the adversary system, which gave to the legal concept of "defense" or "defendant" a physical meaning. Trial by battle was a savage yet sacred method of proof which was also thought to involve divine intercession on behalf of the righteous. Rather than let a wrongdoer triumph, God would presumably strengthen the arms of the party who had sworn truly to the justice of his cause. Right, not might, would therefore conquer. Trial by battle was originally available for the settlement of all disputes, from debt and ownership to robbery and rape, but eventually was restricted to cases of serious crime. In this particular form of proof there was a significant exception to the oral character of the old procedures. The accusation leading to battle, technically known as an "appeal of felony," had to be written, and nothing but the most exact form, giving full particulars of the alleged crime, would be accepted. The indictment, or accusation, by grand jury would later imitate the "appeal" in this respect.

Whether one proved his case by compurgation, ordeal, or battle, the method was accusatory in character. There was always a definite and known accuser, some private person who brought formal suit and openly confronted his antagonist. There was never any secrecy in the proceedings, which were the same for criminal as for civil litigation. The judges, who had no role whatever in the making of the verdict, decided only which party should be put to proof and what its form should be; thereafter the judges merely enforced an observance of the rules. The oaths that saturated the proceedings called upon God to witness to the truth of the respective claims of the parties, or the justice of their cause, or the reliability of their word. No one gave testimonial evidence, nor was anyone questioned to test his veracity.

It was the inquest, a radically different proceeding, that eventually supplanted the old forms of proof while borrowing their accusatorial character. An extraordinarily fertile and versatile device, the inquest was the parent of our double jury system, the grand jury of accusation and the petty jury of trial. Fortunately for the history of freedom, the inquest, a Norman import, was also one of the principal means by which the monarchy developed a centralized government in England. The survival of the inquest was insured by its close ties to royal power and royal prosperity; its particular English form was founded on the old accusatorial procedures. The word "inquest" derives from the Latin *inquisitio*, or inquisition, but beyond the similarity in name shared nothing with the canon law procedure, which became, in fact, its opposite and great rival. The inquest was also known as the *recognitio*, or recognition, which meant a solemn answer or finding or declaration of truth. The inquest was just that, an answer or declaration of truth, a *veri dictum*, or verdict by a body of men from the same neighborhood who were summoned by some official, on the authority of the crown, to reply under oath to any inquiries that might be addressed to them. Men of the same locality were chosen simply because they were most likely to know best the answers to questions relating to the inquest—who had evaded taxes, who owned certain lands, who was suspected of crime, and who knew of misconduct among the king's officers.

At first the inquest was used mainly in administrative and financial inquiries. The Domesday Book, for example, that enormously detailed description or census of landowners, their property down to the last calf and acre, and its cash value, was compiled at least in part by an elaborate inquest for tax assessment purposes. The king's representatives went into the counties in 1086, summoned men from each "hundred," or county subdivision (originally the "hundred" was a hundred households), put them under oath, and demanded their verdicts or truthful answers concerning who owned what and how much. After an abortive attempt by Henry I to establish a system of resident judges, royal commissioners periodically went on circuit, or "eyre," throughout the country to transact the king's business. In the passage of time they undertook duties that became increasingly judicial. They inspected the provinces, gathered revenues and information, occasionally heard lawsuits, and superintended the local details of the king's government. They also aided the exchequer's fiscal business by assessing taxes, holding sheriffs and other revenue collectors to account, and inquiring into the proprietary rights of the crown.

Financial and executive business was similarly conducted with the help of inquests, which increasingly involved the itinerant royal commissioners in matters connected with the administration of justice. The king had a stake not only in suits that concerned his royal domain and his own litigation; he looked to all fines, amercements, escheats, and forfeitures of every sort to contribute to his royal revenues, including the profits that might accrue from purely private suits. He claimed, for example, the goods of felons; not only did he acquire the chattels of a condemned man who had been defeated in battle by private appeal of felony; the king had a right, too, to plunder his lands for a year or sell off that right to a local lord. As Sir James Fitzjames Stephen said, "The rigorous enforcement of all the proprietary and other profitable rights of the Crown which the articles of eyre confided to the justices was naturally associated with their duties as administrators of the criminal law, in which the King was deeply interested, not only because it protected the life and property of his subjects, but also because it contributed to his revenues." Thus the king's traveling justices were a major factor in the early centralization of England, and their most useful instrument became the inquest in matters both civil and criminal.

What was an irregular and in some respects an extraordinary procedure became under King Henry II (1154–1189) normal and systematic. A man of powerful will, administrative genius, and reforming spirit, Henry II greatly increased the jurisdiction of the royal courts, and wherever they traveled on eyre through the kingdom, the inquest followed. Henry II disliked and distrusted the traditional forms of proof. More boldly than his predecessors, he regarded breaches of peace or threats to life and limb as offenses of a public nature, warranting more than merely private retribution. Crimes of a serious nature he took to be offenses against the king's peace, requiring settlement in the king's courts by the king's system of justice, whenever possible, rather than by the older proofs only; and the king's system was founded on the inquest, the representative verdict of the neighborhood. What was once only an administrative inquiry became the foundation of the jury of accusation and the jury of trial in both civil and criminal matters.

Older forms of proof or trial were becoming corrupted, their irrationality apparent to the new, university-trained royal administrators. Compurgation, having hardly survived the Conquest in criminal matters, was the most untrustworthy. It had become too easy a proof, almost a certain success for the party, however culpable or liable, who was lucky enough to be awarded the right to resort to his oath with the support of oath-helpers. They swore only to their belief that his oath was reliable, no longer to their knowledge that it was in fact true. Compurgators who had become little more than character witnesses could no longer be punished for perjury, making the procedure pretty much a ritualistic farce. Moreover, the oaths of compurgators seemed inconsistent with the oaths of the sworn inquest, a much more impartial body.

Henry II placed little more trust in ordeals than he did in compurgation; they were too easily manipulated by the priests who administered them. Nevertheless, as sanctified ceremonials, ordeals were not easily dispensable, and they were both quick and profitable to the crown. Ordeal by battle, however, was too dangerous—not only to life and limb but to the security of vested interests—to endure without providing an alternate form of proof for the settlement of disputes. Battle was also becoming too inequitable and farcical. In civil cases, such as disputes over property, the employment of champions, which was once exceptional, had become routine. Champions were hired to do battle on behalf of a litigant whenever one of the parties was unable, for reasons of age, sex, or physical infirmity, to represent himself. The champion was at first a witness who could prove the case of the litigant, but in time champions became professional fighters available for hire in all civil cases, regardless of the physical capacity of the party. Sometimes champions were used to get rid of gangs of criminals.

Henry II did not abolish older forms of proof; he sought, instead, to supersede them in as many instances as possible, by

discrediting them and by making available to litigants an alternative and more equitable form of proceeding. The Innovations
began in 1164 when the Constitutions of Clarendon prescribed
the use of a recognition by twelve sworn men to decide any
dispute between laymen and clergy on the question whether
land was subject to lay or clerical tenure. The Constitutions of
Clarendon provided also that laymen should not be sued in ecclesiastical courts on untrustworthy or insufficient evidence,
but that if the suspect were someone whom no one might dare
to accuse, the sheriff on the request of the bishop must swear a
jury of twelve to declare the truth by bringing the accusation.
In the Constitutions of Clarendon, then, one sees the glim-
mering of the civil jury in cases of land disputes and of the
grand jury of criminal presentment or accusation.

The Assize, or ordinance, of Clarendon, which Henry II
promulgated two years later, on the centennial of the Conquest, provided for the firm foundation of the grand jury and
instituted a variety of significant procedural reforms. The king
instructed the royal judges on circuit, or eyre, to take jurisdiction over certain serious crimes or felonies presented to them
by sworn inquests, the representative juries of the various localities. Twelve men from each hundred of the county and four
from each vill or township of the hundred were to be summoned by the sheriff to attend the public eyre. They were en-
joined to inquire into all crimes since the beginning of Henry
II's reign, and to report under oath all persons accused or suspected by the vicinage. The parties who were thus presented,
if not already in custody, would be arrested and put to the ordeal of cold water. Even if absolved, those of very bad reputa-

tion were forced to leave the realm. In certain cases, then, mere presentment was tantamount to a verdict of banishment, but generally was not more than an accusation that was tried by ordeal. The Assize of Northampton, issued in 1176, recodified the Assize of Clarendon, extended the list of felonies, and substituted maiming for hanging as the punishment of the accused felon who was "undone" at the ordeal; he also lost a foot, his right hand, his chattels, and was banished. In actuality he usually fled to the forest if he could to live as an outlaw to escape the ordeal or banishment. The Assize of 1176 made permanent, at least at the pleasure of the king, the revised procedure of accusation by twelve knights of the hundred or twelve freemen of the hundred and four of the vill.

The Assizes of Clarendon and Northampton, by establishing what became the grand jury, offered a royally sanctioned option to the old system of private accusations by appeals of felony. Trial by battle, which was begun by an "appeal of felony" in criminal cases, continued, but it was undermined by the king's jury of criminal presentment as the model way of beginning a criminal trial. Henry II also made available an escape from trial by battle in cases begun by an appeal of felony. On the theory that the security of the king's peace could not be safely left to accusations brought by private initiative, many of which were motivated by malice, the writ *de odio et atia*, "of spite and hatred," was provided for appellees. For a price, the writ could be obtained from the king's court by one who claimed that his appellor proceeded from spite and hatred. A jury of recognitors would then be impaneled to render a verdict on this plea; if the jury sustained it, the appeal was quashed and battle avoided. What was in essence a jury's verdict was therefore substituted in some instances for trial by battle. Nevertheless, the trial jury in criminal cases was unknown during the twelfth century. The trial jury in civil cases developed first, providing a model that could later be copied in criminal cases.

Reform of the machinery of civil justice at the expense of trial by battle was one of Henry II's foremost achievements. Once again his instrument was the sworn inquest or jury. Its use in cases of property disputes contributed to the stability of land tenures, extended the jurisdiction of the royal courts at the expense of the feudal courts, aided the cause of justice at the same time that fees for the privilege of using the royal courts contributed to the king's exchequer, and sapped trial by battle in civil cases. The Constitutions of Clarendon in 1164 provided the precedent for turning to twelve men of the countryside for a verdict on a question concerning property rights. Such questions, especially in relation to the possession and title of land, produced the most common and surely the most important civil actions. For their solution Henry II gradually introduced what became the trial jury.

In 1166 the assize of *novel disseisin*, or recent dispossession, established the principle that no one might be evicted or dispossessed of his land without the approval of a jury verdict. This assize created a legal remedy for one who had been dispossessed. He could obtain a writ commanding the sheriff to summon twelve freemen of the vicinity who presumably knew the facts of the case, put them under oath, and then in the presence of the itinerant royal judges require them to render a verdict on the question whether the tenant had been dispossessed.

A verdict in the tenant's favor restored him to possession of his land. If, however, a lord seized the land of a tenant who died before the tenant's heirs might take possession of it, the assize of *novel disseisin* provided no remedy. The assize of *mort d'ancestor*, instituted in 1176, did so. The heir might obtain a writ that put before a jury the question whether the decedent died in possession of the land and whether the claimant was his rightful heir. In the same reign, the assize of *darrein presentment* provided for a verdict by jury on questions involving rival claims to the possession of certain "advowsons," or ecclesiastical benefices, which were regarded as a form of real estate.

Possession, though often indicative of right, was not synonymous with it. One might hold land without having title to it. The dispossessor, not the dispossessed, might be the rightful owner; the heir might have a defective title. Thus settlement of the question of possession was merely provisional, for it left the main question of ownership undecided, and that question was settled by battle. The claimant obtained a writ of right, the civil analogue to the appeal of felony in criminal cases, and challenged the possessor to a duel, with both parties represented by champions. But Henry II's Grand Assize, which was introduced in 1179, opened the way to peaceable settlement. The challenged party, in any case involving a question of proprietary right, might obtain a counterwrit, transferring jurisdiction to the royal courts; he thereby consented to have the question settled by a jury which was chosen with great care to ensure disinterestedness. The sheriff selected four knights, who in turn chose twelve others of the same neighborhood where the land was located, and the twelve, mainly from their own knowledge, declared which party had the better right to the land. Ranulf de Glanville, chief justice to Henry II, overpraised the procedure of the Grand Assize as a "royal benefit whereby life and property are so wholesomely cared for that men can avoid the chance of the combat and yet keep whatever they have in their freeholds."

By the time of Magna Carta in 1215, the inquest in civil cases was becoming fairly well established as the trial jury, though in criminal cases it was scarcely known at all. The petty or possessory assizes of *novel disseisin*, *mort d'ancestor*, and *darrein presentment* had proved to be so popular that chapter eighteen of Magna Carta guaranteed that the circuit court would sit several times a year in each county for the purpose of obtaining verdicts on disputes that they settled. Civil disputes of virtually any description, not merely those named in the petty assizes, might be referred to the verdict of local recognitors if both parties would consent to the procedure.

On the criminal side of the law, Magna Carta in chapter thirty-six provided that the writ *de odio et atia*, which by 1215 had become known as the writ of life and limb, should be granted without charge. It was by no means uncommon by then for a person accused by private appeal to demand a jury verdict on any number of "exceptions," such as the writ of life and limb, in the hope of getting the appeal quashed. In such cases, however, the jury decided only the question whether the "exception" was valid; the main question of guilt or innocence, which the appeal had raised, was still settled by battle if the exception was not sustained. Criminal accusations, which were presented in accord with the grand inquest provided by the Assize of Clarendon, were tried by ordeal. Magna Carta, in chapter twenty-eight, ensured that no one could be put to the ordeal unless formally accused by the jury of presentment before the royal judges on circuit. This was the implication of the provision that "credible witnesses," members of the presenting jury, must corroborate that fact that there had been an indictment. The celebrated chapter twenty-nine did not guarantee trial by jury for the simple reason that its use in criminal cases was still unknown in 1215. At best that chapter ensured that the indictment and trial by whatever was the appropriate test, whether battle or ordeal, must precede sentence.

The course of history was affected at the same time by events in Rome. The Fourth Lateran Council in 1215 forbade the participation of the clergy in the administration of ordeals, thereby divesting that proof of its rationale as a judgment of God. As a result, the ordeal died as a form of trial in western Europe, and some other procedure was needed to take its place. While the continental nations and the church turned to the Inquisition, England found in its own form of the inquest a device at hand that would fill the gap. The absence of heresy in England and therefore of a papal Inquisition allowed the alternative.

With the ordeal abolished, battle remained the only means of trying a criminal case. But the movement of the law was away from battle. The same reasons of "equity" that led Glanville in 1187 to say that the right to a freehold "can scarcely be proved by battle" spurred the search for an alternate means of proving an accusation of crime. Thus Magna Carta had made the writ of life and limb free but still reflected traditional thinking in terms of ordeals and battle. Battle could never be had, however, in cases where one of the parties was aged, crippled, sick, or a woman. With the ordeal gone, England's criminal procedure, in the words of Frederick Pollock and F. W. Maitland, "was deprived of its handiest weapon." Not only was there no way to try those who could not engage in battle; there was the greater quandary of what should be done with persons who had been accused by the sworn verdict of a grand inquest. Battle was possible only in the case of a private appeal of felony. According to Stephen, "When trial by ordeal was abolished and the system of accusation by grand juries was established, absolutely no mode of ascertaining the truth of an accusation made by a grand jury remained." Nevertheless, compurgation and suit by witnesses lingered for a long time.

The crown's bewilderment was revealed in a writ of 1219 giving instructions to the circuit judges: "Because it was in doubt and not definitely settled before the beginning of your eyre, with what trial those are to be judged who are accused of robbery, murder, arson, and similar crimes, since the trial by fire and water has been prohibited by the Roman Church," notorious criminals should be imprisoned, those accused of "medium" crimes who were not likely to offend again should be banished, and those accused of lesser crimes might be released on "pledge of fidelity and keeping our peace." The writ concluded, "We have left to your discretion the observance of this aforesaid order according to your own discretion and conscience," a formula that left the judges further perplexed but free to improvise.

Treating an accusation as a conviction, when an accusation

was little more than an expression of popular opinion, was a makeshift that fell so short of doing justice that it could not survive. In retrospect it seems natural that the judges on circuit should have turned to a sworn inquest for help. An eyre was a great event, virtually a county parliament. Present were the local nobles and bishops, the sheriffs and bailiffs, the knights and freeholders, and a very great many juries. From every hundred of the county there was a jury of twelve men, and from every township four representatives. Surrounded by the various juries, the judge in a criminal case could take the obvious course of seeking the sense of the community. The original jury of presentment was already sworn, presumably knew most about the facts, and was a representative group. The jurors' indictment had not necessarily voiced their own belief in the prisoner's guilt; it rather affirmed the fact that he was commonly suspected. Although practice varied considerably at first, the judges began to ask the jury of presentment to render a verdict of guilty or not guilty on their accusation. Because the jury of presentment was more likely than not to sustain its indictment, even though the jurors had sworn only that the accused was suspected and not that he was guilty, the judges usually swore in the representatives of the surrounding townships and asked whether they concurred; the jury of another hundred might also be conscripted to corroborate the verdict. In effect a body of the countryside gave the verdict.

This practice of enlarging the original jury of presentment or seeking a series of verdicts from different juries was common during the thirteenth century. What became the petty jury was thus initially larger than the grand jury. The practice was too cumbersome, the body too unwieldy. Twelve was the number of the presenting jury and twelve the jury in many civil cases; gradually only twelve jurors were selected to try the indictment, but they always included among their number some of the original jury of presentment. The unfairness inherent in this practice, and the theory that the accused must consent to this jury, eventually led to a complete separation of the grand jury and the trial jury.

Consent, even if induced by coercion, was an ancient feature of accusatory procedure. In Saxon times the accused party had to appear personally before his accuser and the assembled community, and had to agree to submit himself to whatever proof was assigned, or be outlawed. When Henry II introduced the sworn inquest in civil cases, it was available to those who secured a writ requesting it; so, too, parties who sought to escape battle consented to abide by the verdict of a jury under the process of the Grand Assize or of the writ of life and limb. Indeed, in cases where a trial jury was known, it was available only after consent. But no man would be likely to consent to the verdict of accusers if they sought his conviction. And no man, it was thought, should be forced to accept the verdict of accusers; acceptance should be voluntary. While ordeals were still in use, if an accused refused to submit himself to the proof, he was considered to have repudiated the law and might therefore be punished as if he had outlawed himself. But the inquest acting as a trial jury was a novel and extraordinary device, and thus the reasoning that had branded as outlaws those who rejected the ordeal now seemed repugnant when it was applied to a man who refused to put himself to the test of a jury. He might think the jury would not fairly decide, or that his chances of getting a verdict of not guilty, for whatever reasons, were hopeless.

To cope with such cases the law developed in two completely different ways, one barbaric, the other salutary. Before the judges turned to a second jury to decide the question of guilt or innocence, they would ask the accused whether he would submit to the final verdict of the "country," that is, of the inquest of the countryside or whole county. Although most men consented, some did not, quite likely because conviction meant the forfeiture of chattels and goods. In cases of no consent, some judges proceeded with the trial anyway; others treated the prisoner as if he were guilty; but most felt that it was unreasonable to compel a man to submit unless he consented. If he refused to consent, the law was nonplussed, the proceedings stymied. At length, in 1275 a statute supplied the answer: extort his consent. The statute read, "that notorious felons who are openly of evil fame and who refuse to put themselves upon inquests of felony at the suit of the King before his justices, shall be remanded to a hard and strong prison as befits those who refuse to abide by the common law of the land; but this is not to be understood of persons who are taken upon light suspicion." It is noteworthy that the trial jury, here called the inquest of felony, by 1275 is described as the common law of the land. By the same date, incidentally, anyone privately accused of felony might avoid battle if he put himself "upon his country," letting a jury decide the question of guilt or innocence.

The notion of consent to trial by jury incredibly remained the law of the land until 1772. A prisoner who refused to plead to the indictment simply could not be tried, though he was subjected to a peculiar form of torture that was calculated to change his mind. Within a quarter of a century of its introduction in 1275, imprisonment strong and hard (*prison forte et dure*) degenerated into punishment strong and hard (*peine forte et dure*). At first the prisoner was stripped, put in irons on the bare ground in the worst part of the prison, and fed only coarse bread one day and water the next, which was surely cruel enough. Then the refinement of "punishment" was added; he was slowly pressed, spread-eagled on the ground, with as much iron placed upon his body as he could bear "and then more." The punishment by pressing, exposure, and slow starvation continued until the prisoner "put himself upon his country" or died. What made this barbarity so peculiar is that it derived from the admirable though rigid rule that the trial could not proceed without the prisoner's consent; moreover, that the worst felon should have an opportunity to prove his innocence. That is, the purpose of *peine forte et dure* was not to extort a confession but simply to extort a plea; the law did not care whether he pleaded guilty or not guilty, only that he pleaded. In 1772 a new statute provided that a prisoner standing mute to indictment of felony should be treated as if he had been convicted by verdict or confession, thus ending *peine forte et dure*. Not till 1827 was that rule altered to direct the court to enter a plea of not guilty for a prisoner who stood "mute of malice" and refused to plead.

The other path taken by the notion of consent led to the emergence of the petty jury in criminal cases. This was the outcome of permitting the prisoner to challenge members of the presenting jury who were impaneled to serve on his trial jury. Henry de Bracton, writing about 1258, noted that the defendant might object to the inclusion of false and malicious accusers, and John Le Britton, near the end of the thirteenth century, said that he might object if the jurors included enemies who sought his destruction or had been induced to lie by the lord who sought his land "through greediness of the escheat." In 1305 Prince Edward, later Edward II, acting on behalf of a friend who had been indicted for murder, asked the judge to provide a jury that excluded all members of the accusing jury. With increasing frequency defendants challenged petty jurors who had first served as their indictors, though the king's justices resisted the challenges because indictors were more likely to convict. For that very reason in the 1340s the Commons twice protested against the inclusion of indictors, but it was not until 1352 that the king agreed to a statute that gave the accused a right to challenge members of the petty jury who had participated in his indictment. As a result of this statute, the two juries became differentiated in composition and function. From about 1376 the custom of requiring a unanimous verdict from twelve petty jurors developed; by that time the size of the grand jury had been fixed at twenty-three, a majority of whom decided whether accusations should be proffered.

By the middle of the fifteenth century, criminal trials were being conducted by rational principles that seem quite modern. Although the law of evidence was still in its rudimentary stages, the trial jury was no longer regarded as a band of witnesses, men who of their own knowledge or from knowledge immediately available from the neighborhood, might swear to the guilt or innocence of the accused. The jury was beginning to hear evidence that was produced in court, though the jurors still continued to obtain facts by their own inquiry. As late as the 1450s it was common for the jurors to visit a witness at his home in the country to take his testimony, but they were also beginning to pass judgment on evidence given in their presence in court. More important, they were regarded as a body of objective men, triers of fact, whose verdict was based on the truth as best they could determine it.

According to the romanticized view of Chief Justice John Fortescue in the mid-fifteenth century, an innocent man need fear nothing because "none but his neighbors, men of honest and good repute, against whom he can have no probable cause of exception, can find the person accused guilty." The accused was no doubt additionally assured because he might challenge without cause as many as thirty-five potential jurors. Witnesses for the crown—the accused was allowed none—gave evidence "in open court," wrote Fortescue, "in the presence and hearing of a jury, of twelve men, persons of good character, neighbors where the fact was committed, apprised of the circumstances in question, and well acquainted with the lives and conversations of the witnesses, especially as they be near neighbors, and cannot but know whether they be worthy of credit, or not." Of course, trial by the local community could be trial by local prejudice, but at least the prisoner knew the charges against him, confronted his accuser, and had freedom to give his own explanations as well as question and argue with the prosecution's witnesses. He suffered from many disadvantages—lack of counsel, lack of witnesses on his own behalf, lack of time to prepare his defense—yet the trial was supremely fair, judged by any standard known in the Western world of that day.

The year 1215, which is celebrated in Anglo-American history because of the signing of Magna Carta, is notable too for an ecclesiastical event of sinister import: the regulations of the Fourth Lateran Council in Rome. The one event ultimately symbolized the liberties of the subject; the other, ultimately, the rack and the *auto-da-fé*. The council was dominated by an imperious autocrat, Pope Innocent III, who chartered a new course for the criminal procedure of the canon law. The church in the thirteenth century and long after was a world power, the only world power, and Innocent III (1198–1216) was more than its head; he was its master. One of the great legislators of the canon law, he was also the scourge of heretics, the man responsible for the Albigensian Crusade, which slaughtered thousands, and for starting the Holy Inquisition on its bloody path. As John H. Wigmore said, Innocent III—a name scarcely apt— "established the inquisition of heresy, by warrants extending into every corner of Europe, a form of terrorism which served to extirpate those who dissented from the Church's dogmas for the next four centuries." The same pope, a maker and breaker of kings, wielded a political authority over the whole of Christendom and sovereignty over its temporal monarchs. It was Innocent III who absolved King John for assenting to Magna Carta, which he thought shameful and detrimental, and for a time he reduced England to the status of a vassal of the papacy. Under his leadership the Fourth Lateran Council defined the attitude of the church toward heretics, the obligations of secular authorities to exterminate them, and a new code of crimi-

nal procedures that incorporated both the *inquisitio*, precursor of
the Holy Inquisition, and a new oath that was self-incriminatory in nature.

The *inquisitio*, originating in the decrees of Innocent III at
the close of the twelfth century and the beginning of the thirteenth, triggered a steady transition in the canon law from the
old accusatorial procedure to the new inquisitorial procedures.
In English law, however, the inquest had led to the double jury
system; in canon law and in the civil law—the secular law of
continental nations, which followed the lead of the church—
the inquest took a completely different form, one that left a trail
of mangled bodies, shattered minds, and smoking flesh. The inquisitional procedure, which at first was aimed at discovering
and punishing misconduct among the clergy, was speedily
adapted to the overweening need of preserving the faith against
heresy. As late as the twelfth century, however, the church had
an equivocal policy toward heretics, a substantially accusatorial
system of criminal procedure, and an abhorrence of some of the
very features that shortly proved most characteristic of the Inquisition. Heresy, an error of faith, was not yet a crime of mental state or conscience; or, rather, only external acts of worship
or doctrinal differences were punished as heresy, and the
church possessed no special machinery for detecting the guilty,
let alone those with guilty thoughts or secret doubts. Back in
the fifth century, Saints Chrysostom and Augustine, although
urging the suppression of heresy, spoke against the death
penalty, against torture, and against forcing men to accuse
themselves. One should confess his sins to God, said Chrysostom: "I do not say to thee, make a parade of thyself, nor accuse

thyself before others." These views were endorsed by the emperor Gratian's *Decretum* in the mid-twelfth century. Gratian espoused the penalties of exile and fine for heretics, repudiated torture, and declared, like Chrysostom, "I say not that thou shouldst incriminate thyself publicly nor accuse thyself before others." As late as 1184 Pope Lucius III merely excommunicated obstinate heretics and turned them over to the secular authority for severe penalties—exile, and confiscation of their properties, destruction of their houses, and loss of all rights. But the penalties did not touch the persons of the guilty; they were neither physically harmed nor imprisoned.

By the mid-thirteenth century, however, all had changed, because of the need of the church to defend itself against the dangers of mass heresy. Thomas Aquinas required truthful answers to incriminating questions and advocated death for heretics in order to save the faith from their corruption; and Pope Innocent IV explicitly sanctioned the use of torture. In the period between Gratian and Aquinas, heresies had spread alarmingly, especially in the South of France among the Cathari, and the faith had found a champion, Pope Innocent III, who used his spiritual sword and administrative genius, however malevolent, to smite the enemies of Christ. Innocent III heralded a new attitude toward heretics. He considered their crime as the most execrable, the most damnable of all, *crimen laesae majestatis divinae* or "high treason against God." In comparison with this crime, Sodom and Gomorrah seemed pure, the infidelity of the Jews seemed justified, and the worst sins seemed holy. The Christian's highest duty was to help exterminate heretics by denouncing them to the ecclesiastical authorities, regardless of any familial or human bonds. The son who did not deliver up his parents, or the wife her husband shared the heretic's guilt. Faithfulness to a heretic, according to Innocent III, was faithlessness to God. The living must die; the guilty who were already dead, if buried in consecrated ground, must be dug up, cursed, and burned.

The procedures available to the church for the discovery and prosecution of heretics were archaic and ineffective before the reforms of Innocent III. In the main these procedures were of the same primitive accusatory character as those employed by the secular authorities in England and on the Continent during the early Middle Ages. Private accusation led to exculpation by the oath of the party, supported by compurgators (the *purgatio canonica*) or by ordeal (the *purgatio vulgaris*). In addition the church very early resorted to an inquest by synodal witnesses which, as Adhemar Esmein observed, culminated in an inquisitional procedure that was "the anti-type of the 'inquisitio' from which sprang the England grand jury." In this ecclesiastical inquest, the bishop, who was the ecclesiastical judge, on visiting a parish within his jurisdiction, would convene a synod or gathering of the faithful. He selected some and swore them to denounce all persons guilty of offenses requiring investigation; then he closely interrogated the denouncers, or synodal witnesses, to uncover malefactors and test the reliability of their testimony. It was but a short step for the ecclesiastical judge to conduct the prosecution against the accused and to decide on his guilt or innocence. Innocent III took that step, which the Fourth Lateran Council confirmed.

The remodeled criminal procedures of the canon law, after

1215, described three modes of prosecution. The first, the *accusatio*, was the traditional form. A private person, on the basis of some information or evidence available to him, voluntarily accused another and thereby became a party to the prosecution, taking upon himself the task of proof. He also took upon himself the risk of being punished in the event that the prosecution failed. The second form of prosecution was the *denunciatio*, which enabled the private accuser to avoid the danger and burden of the *accusatio*. Either an individual or the synodal witnesses played the role of informer, secretly indicting or denouncing someone before the court. The judge himself then became a party to the suit *ex officio*, by virtue of his office, and conducted the prosecution for the secret accuser. The third form was the *inquisitio*, by which the judge combined in his person all roles—that of accuser, prosecutor, judge, and jury. Technically the judge could not institute a suit unless an important preliminary condition had first been met: he must satisfy himself that there were probable grounds for the *inquisitio*. This was the canon law's equivalent of the grand jury of presentment of the English common law. The canon law required that an accusation must rest on *infamia*, infamy or bad reputation, which was established by the existence of either notorious suspicion (*clamosa insinuatio*) or common report (*fama*), which was some sort of public rumor. But the inquisitor himself, supposedly a wise and incorruptible man, was the sole judge of the existence of *infamia*, and his own suspicions, however based or baseless, were also adequate for the purpose of imprisoning the suspect and putting him to an inquisition. The Fourth Lateran Council prescribed no form for the establishment of *infamia* if the judge decided to proceed *ex officio mero*, of his own accord or at his discretion.

CHAPTER II

※

Inquisitorial versus Accusatorial Procedures

Dᴜʀɪɴɢ ᴛʜᴇ ɪɴϙᴜɪsɪᴛɪᴏɴ, the ecclesiastical judge became a law unto himself, operating in secrecy. Every defense was trammeled, every avenue of escape closed, leaving the accused at the complete mercy of his judge, the inquisitor. The role of the judicial inquisitor and the nature of the crime that he sought to establish and punish explain the severe procedures of the Inquisition as well as its gross atrocities. The judge was commissioned to perform a sacred mission, to avenge God and purify the faith by extirpating the ultimate sin, the heresy of disbelief or doubt. He was not merely a judge of overt acts of crime; as father-confessor to his victim, he also sought to extract from him a confession of his guilt so that his soul might be saved despite his wanton or ignorant errors of conscience that could lead only to eternal damnation. The inquisitor's task, therefore, in the words of Henry Charles Lea, was the nearly impossible one "of ascertaining the secret thoughts and opinions of the prisoner. [T]he believer must have fixed and unwavering faith, and it was the inquisitor's business to ascertain this condition of his mind."

The defendant's behavior proved little except outward conformity, and that might be illusory, certainly inconclusive proof of the "most unbounded submission to the decision of the Holy See, the strictest adherence to orthodox doctrine, the freest readiness to subscribe to whatever was demanded of him." Despite his verbal professions, his regularity at mass, his punctuality at confession, he might be a heretic at heart, fit only for the stake. His guilt was an unquestioned presumption which could lead only to a foregone conclusion, his condemnation. Legal niceties, procedural regularities, and forms of law counted for little when the objective was to obtain a conviction at any cost in order to fulfill a sacred mission.

On the other hand, the canon law, influenced by the Roman law of the later empire, developed a highly sophisticated system of evidence, later known as the theory of legal proofs, which supposedly would help the accused by preventing the conviction of the innocent. The theory of legal proofs functioned as the canon law's equivalent of trial by jury to insure acquittal of the innocent and conviction of the guilty. The burden of proof, as in the accusatory system of old, was wholly upon the accuser or prosecutor, but the canon law required an unusual degree of proof in both kind and quantity. Innocent III, for example, cautioned inquisitors against convicting on merely "violent presumptions" in a matter as heinous as heresy. What the canon law required was perfect or complete proof that in a later day was specified with considerable complexity and quasi-scientific exactness. Complete proof was a proof clearer than the sun at midday. It consisted, ideally, of the testimony of two eyewitnesses, neither impeached nor impeachable, to the same fact; they must have seen the prisoner commit the crime in order to complete the proof in a capital case. Proof so stringent and certain was nearly impossible to procure, especially when the crime was essentially one of thought. Documentary evidence, such as heretical writings, carried weight but was rarely available. "Proximate indications" or "half proofs," such as many hearsay witnesses, and weighty presumptions or conjectural proofs were insufficient to support a conviction. The prisoner's confession was needed for corroboration.

The tyranny of the system of legal proofs, together with the inquisitor's zeal to snatch a soul from Satan, led irresistibly to the tyranny of the Inquisition, in which the confession became the crux of the trial and prevented the development of anything remotely comparable to a jury. The secret interrogation, the requirement of a self-incriminatory oath, and, finally, the employment of torture had as their single objective the confession of the prisoner. "The accused," reported Bernard Gui, one of the leading inquisitors of the early fourteenth century, "are not to be condemned unless they confess or are convicted by witnesses, though not according to the ordinary laws, as in other crimes, but according to the private laws or privileges conceded to the inquisitors by the Holy See, for there is much that is peculiar to the Inquisition." The judge who was convinced of his prisoner's guilt but lacked the necessary proof was driven to extort a confession by any means, however re-

33

pulsive. In the interest of defending the faith, the most unspeakable punishments were sanctioned. The Inquisition was the classic case of the ends justifying the means. In 1252 Innocent IV issued his bull, *Ad extirpanda*, directing the establishment of machinery for systematic persecution and authorizing the use of torture. The bull empowered the civil authorities to torture suspects in order to force them to name their accomplices as well as to confess their own guilt of heresy. Four years later the pope authorized ecclesiastical judges to absolve one another and mutually grant dispensation for "irregularities," thereby enabling them to administer torture directly.

Confessions extorted by torture had to be "freely" repeated after torture; in the event of a retraction by the prisoner, he was returned to the rack for a "continuance." Torture certainly was an efficacious system of interrogation, saving time and trouble for the inquisitors, but they had other means of persuading the prisoner to confess. He could be imprisoned indefinitely, often for years, in a dark dungeon, in solitary confinement, and be kept half starved, frozen, and sleepless, incapable of defending himself when brought before the inquisitor for a fresh interrogation.

The usual course of a trial, which consisted of the secret examination of the accused under oath, was to confront him with the mass of surmises and rumors and hearsay against him and demand his confession. The indictment was built from the testimony of secret informers, malicious gossips, self-confessed victims, and frightened witnesses who, anxious to save themselves from being racked, revealed from their frantic imaginations whatever they thought the inquisitor might wish to hear.

Convicted heretics whose infamy disqualified them as witnesses in all other cases, gave the most prized testimony in heresy cases, but they could testify for the prosecution only. A prisoner who confessed, abjured heresy, and proclaimed his penitence could prove his sincerity and escape the stake, if not by prison, by betraying friends, neighbors, and family. Guile, deceit, entrapment, promises, threats, and, if necessary, the rack managed inevitably to triumph. Lea reported that the entire history of the Inquisition reveals not a single instance of complete acquittal. Everyone who appeared before the Inquisition was put to some form of penance, at the very least. In sum, "Abandon hope, all ye who enter here" best described the chances of an accused person under the inquisitorial system of criminal procedure that operated throughout the Continent. The church had been the first authority to switch to the inquisitorial system from the accusatorial, and its supreme example speedily inspired European nations, excepting England, to reform the procedures of their secular criminal law in Rome's image. Everywhere the secret examination, the inquisitional oath, and torture became the standard, at first used only in "extraordinary" cases but quickly degenerated into a completely routine procedure for all cases but the most petty. Thus trial by jury was unknown on the Continent.

The English system, based on the presentment by grand jury, the written indictment, and trial by jury, differed most markedly from the continental system in the roles played by the judge and the jury. In the case of a felony, the officers of a French court, like the ecclesiastical judge in a case of heresy, completely dominated the proceedings at every stage from arrest to verdict. The English judge, by contrast, remained essentially a referee of a private fight, enforcing the observance of the rules by both parties, thus ensuring a more objective verdict by a trial jury. As an appointee of the crown, the English judge was naturally partial to the prosecution and by his conduct often showed his favoritism, but he had neither a personal nor an official stake in the outcome of a criminal proceeding and little ability to command a verdict of guilty from the jury. He had no authority whatever to initiate or promote a prosecution, nor to make an accusation of crime against anyone.

In the inquisitorial system, the accusation and prosecution rested entirely with the court, which was also the accuser, to the extent that any accuser was known. He was in a sense nameless and faceless, hidden beneath a hood that was called *fama* or *clamosa insinuatio*—common report or notorious suspicion. In England the name of the accuser had to be as definite as the accusation itself. The accuser was a witness who instigated the prosecution, and his direct and open participation in the case was indispensable. Unless an officer of the crown of his own knowledge suspected a man's guilt, he could not make an arrest without the sworn complaint or the physical presence of the witness who brought the accusation. The witness himself, as a matter of fact, had virtually the same powers of arrest as a crown officer. Without the accuser there could not even be a prosecution. A suspect might confess his guilt to a justice of the peace at a preliminary examination, be indicted by a grand jury, and yet plead not guilty at his arraignment, perhaps because he planned to retract the confession at his trial before a petty jury. When the trial opened, if his accuser was not present to testify against him, or if the justice of the peace, to whom he had confessed, did not testify either, "although the malefactor hath confessed the crime to the justice of the peace, and that it appear by his hand and confirmation," wrote Sir Thomas Smith about 1565, "the twelve men will acquit the prisoner." The accuser's role was so vital that he even had the same power of prosecution as a crown attorney. In England and in England alone the prosecution of crimes, in Stephen's words, was "left entirely to private persons, or to public officers who act in their capacity of private persons and who hardly have any legal powers beyond those which belong to private persons." By contrast, wherever the inquisitorial procedure prevailed, the court or its officers were alone empowered to institute accusations and prosecutions. Every criminal case was an official inquiry into the guilt or innocence of the accused. Moreover, the grand and petty juries served to bring and try accusations.

In England and England only, the grand jury made the formal presentment of crime against the accused on the basis of information originally known personally to its members, and the crown attorney framed an indictment accordingly; or the attorney, on the basis of any accusation brought to his attention, drew the bill of indictment for the grand jury's verdict, and if the evidence indicated the suspect's guilt, the grand jury approved of the indictment. Without its approval, however, there could be no prosecution for treason or felony. The judge had no part in the bringing of the presentment, the framing of the indictment, or the verdict of the grand jury. The grand jury not only stood between the suspect and the government that sought to prosecute him; the judge himself subjected the indictment to the most exacting scrutiny. It was the only written document in the entire proceedings, which were in all other respects oral.

The indictment inherited the characteristics of the old appeal of felony by private accusers seeking satisfaction by battle. It had to be a rigorously formal document that met every exacting technicality of the law, describing the accusation with the utmost particularity and accuracy. The specific crime charged against the accused and the time, place, and manner of its commission had to be precisely defined. Although the English common law recognized such vague crimes as seditious libel, conspiracy, and compassing the death of the king, it was generally inhospitable to dragnet definitions, which jeopardized personal security, and to crimes of mental state, such as heresy. The courts demanded strictness in indictments and treated the crown as if it were scarcely more than a private appellor bringing an appeal of felony, though every indictment was framed in the name of the king.

Such strictness threw upon the crown the obligation of stating and proving its case in a manner unknown to a court of the inquisitorial system, which knew no such thing as the rule of law enforceable even against the sovereign. There was no security whatsoever against the arbitrary power of an inquisitor of the church or a French magistrate. They were not even required to notify a prisoner of the crimes charged against him, let alone when, where, and how he was alleged to have committed them. The English judge had no discretion in such matters; his continental counterpart was governed by discretion alone. In England the entire indictment was read to the prisoner, who was free to make exceptions on grounds of law, though without the aid of counsel. The judge, at least in theory, served as his counsel, and on questions relating to the sufficiency of the indictment or informing him of the charges against him, the theory was realistic. The English jury, however, functioned independently of the judge, and only the jury's verdict mattered.

The English judge presided over a criminal trial that was a symbolic reenactment of the old trial by battle. The proceeding was adversary in nature, and though the crown possessed several important advantages, its position was like that of the plaintiff in a civil case. Indeed, a criminal prosecution resembled in most respects the most ordinary litigation between private parties disputing the title to an estate. The trial was preeminently litigious, following substantially the same rules of procedure and pleadings as a civil trial. The defendant was completely free to make his defense as best he could, and he was tried publicly and before a jury—advantages of inestimable value compared to a secret inquisition. Again, the role of the English judge is most significant; he was in the main an impassive observer. It was not his duty to collect evidence against the prisoner, to evaluate it, to interrogate him—though he could do so, of course—or to judge him. In a sense the trial jury was the real judge. The English judge was neither accuser nor prosecutor; he conducted no inquest against the defendant, was not a party adverse to him, and rendered no verdicts. Without reason to be powerfully biased against him, to strain for a conviction, or to presume guilt, the judge could afford to be neutral, or at least relatively fair. The jury allowed the English judge to avoid becoming an inquisitor.

Nevertheless, English judges of the Middle Ages tended to be harsh and sometimes abused the defendant with scornful remarks; but they were comparatively just. The crown's attorney had the task of conducting the prosecution and proving to a jury his case against the prisoner. The trial was a running argument between prosecution and defense, as if they were engaged in a combat before the jury. The examination of the defendant was the focus of the proceeding. If the defendant had the wit and the tongue, he could give as well as he got from counsel against him, disputing and denying point for point, calling for production of the evidence, criticizing it, demanding to be confronted with the state's witnesses or to see their depositions. As Stephen says, "The trials were short and sharp; they were directed to the very point at issue, and whatever disadvantages the prisoner lay under, he was allowed to say whatever he pleased; his attention was pointedly called to every part of the case against him, and if he had a real answer to make he had the opportunity to bring it out effectively and in detail. It was but seldom that he was abused or insulted." The judge ruled on points of law and, when the oral combat was over, summed up the evidence for the benefit of the jury and instructed it on the law that governed the case. The jury was then free to decide as it pleased on the question of guilt or innocence.

The entire proceeding stood in merciful contrast to the inquisitorial procedure, which cast the judge in every role and in every one as an implacable enemy of his victim. Lea's remark about the spirit that infected an inquisitor of the canon law applies with equal force to an inquisitor of the French royal court: he conducted himself as if "the sacrifice of a hundred innocent men were better than the escape of one guilty." By contrast, the humanity of the English judge even in an age of cruelty persuaded him that the cause of justice was best served by bending over backward to avoid convicting the innocent. As early as 1302 it was said in England that the best course was to relinquish the punishment of a wrongdoer rather than punish the innocent. Chief Justice John Fortescue, in the mid-fifteenth century, expressed a standard that became a maxim of English law: "Indeed, one would much rather that twenty guilty persons should escape the punishment of death, than that one innocent person should be condemned, and suffer capitally." A century and a half later even the Star Chamber professed to believe in the maxim that "it were better to acquit twenty that are guilty than condemn one innocent."

The humanity of the English judge was above all marked by his abhorrence of torture. The horrible punishment meted out to a prisoner who refused to plead either guilty or not guilty was undoubtedly a form of torture, yet *peine forte et dure* was never imposed except to force one to consent to being tried by a jury. It was never employed to extort a confession or to force the prisoner to incriminate himself in any manner. It was the proud boast of the English judge that torture was illegal in a common-law proceeding. Fortescue's panegyric of English law turned him to French law again and again for a chauvinistic comparison. The French, he said, do not think it enough to convict the accused by evidence, lest the innocent should thereby be condemned; they choose, rather, to put the accused to the rack "till they confess their guilt, rather than rely entirely on the depositions of witnesses, who, very often, from unreasonable prejudice and passion, sometimes, at the instigation of wicked men, are suborned, and so become guilty of perjury. By which overcautious, and inhuman stretch of policy, the suspected, as well as the really guilty, are in that kingdom, tortured in so many ways, as is too tedious and bad for description. Some are extended on the rack, till their very sinews crack, and the veins gush out in streams of blood: others have weights hung to their feet, till their limbs are almost torn asunder, and the whole body dislocated: some have their mouths gagged to such a wideness, for a long time, whereat such quantities of water are poured in, that their bellies swell to prodigious degree, and then being pierced with a faucet, spigot, or other instrument for the purpose, the water spouts out in great abundance, like a whale. To describe the inhumanity of such exquisite tortures affects me with too real a concern, and varieties of them are not to be recounted in a large volume." Other kingdoms, added Fortescue, similarly engaged in torture: "now, what man is there so stout or resolute, who had once gone through this horrid trial by torture, be he never so innocent, who will not rather confess himself guilty of all kinds of wickedness, than undergo like tortures a second time? Who would not rather die once, since death would put an end to all his fears, than to be killed so many times, and suffer so many hellish tortures, more terrible than death itself?"

Torture thrived in dark and secret places but could not survive a public trial before a jury. Secrecy, having infected the entire inquisitorial process, brutalized its judges. They cited, arrested, accused, imprisoned, collected evidence, examined, prosecuted, tortured, convicted, and punished—all in secrecy. Only the final sentence was publicized. By contrast, publicity bathed the English common-law procedure, at least through the mid-sixteenth century. Criminal procedure under the Tudors took on a definite inquisitorial cast, though it remained essentially accusatorial and juries could acquit a person accused by a Tudor prosecutor. The unsettling effect of the Reformation in England, intensified by the conflicting religious policies of succeeding sovereigns, and frequent riots, rebellious factions, and general disorders motivated the Tudors to increase the surveillance of the central government over the entire country by stricter police control. Torture, ordered by the Privy Council, and an inquisitorial examination of suspects entered into English practice, though torture was undoubtedly used on a sporadic basis as early as the fifteenth century. When Sir Thomas Smith later wrote that torture "to put a malefactor to excessive paine, to make him confesse himselfe, or of his felowes or complices, is not used in England," he meant that it was not used at common law, which featured judgments by trial juries. The opinion of the common-law judges was that torture was illegal. But it could be employed, and was, by the special command or authority of the king in his prerogative courts. It was an extraordinary power of the crown that might be inflicted in extraordinary cases, at first only those involving the safety of the state; but its brutalizing effect on those who practiced it and its unquestionable efficiency led inevitably to its use in cases of serious crime that were unrelated to state security. Yet the use of torture, which continued until approximately 1650, was always restricted to the Privy Council and its judicial arm, the Court of Star Chamber.

The principal incursion made by the inquisitorial system on the common law itself was the preliminary examination of accused persons. In 1554 and 1555 Parliament enacted statutes that were intended to safeguard against collusion between justices of the peace and criminal suspects whom they too freely bailed. This legislation, as it turned out, had the effect of increasing the efficiency of criminal procedure by filling an important gap. Grand jurors had lost their character as presenters of the names of those who were reputed publicly to be criminals, and grand jurors were also losing their character as witnesses who of their own knowledge suspected certain persons of crime. More and more, grand jurors were becoming dependent upon the production of evidence before them by crown officers. Justices of the peace, those county officials who have been called the government's "men-of-all-work" and whose duties included police and administrative functions as well as judicial functions, were authorized by the acts of 1554 and 1555 to take the examination of all persons suspected of crime and of their accusers.

By the close of the sixteenth century these examinations were becoming quite inquisitorial. The suspect was closely and strictly interrogated in private; his accusers and witnesses against him were examined out of his presence, and their evidence was withheld from him until the trial. The purpose of examining the suspect was to trap him into a confession. Torture, however, as has been indicated, was never used in any

common-law proceeding. Nevertheless, the preliminary examination by the justice of the peace was a common-law equivalent of the secret inquisition used on the Continent. Moreover,
any damaging admissions made by the suspect were produced
against him at his trial before a jury. The record of the examination was usually introduced in evidence at the beginning of
the trial, placing the defendant in an unfavorable light, to say
the least. Fortunately the trial itself, even before the Star Chamber, remained public, and the defendant could always retract or
deny compromising statements made to the justice of the
peace. Neither in the preliminary examination nor in the trial
was the defendant required or permitted to make statements
under oath. The requirement of a public trial by a jury and the
minimal role of the trial judge saved English procedure from
degenerating into an inquisitorial system. That the court was
open to all who cared to attend, the interested and the curious,
made a difference; but it was the authority of the trial jury that
finally counted, not merely in the disposition of any case but
in the retention of the accusatory system.

Despite the preliminary examination by the justice of the
peace, the indictment by the grand jury, the evidence submitted by the crown, and the instructions of the judge, the trial
jurors when locked up to reach a verdict were responsible only
to their own consciences. They were completely free to return
a verdict of their pleasure in accordance with what they
thought right. The evidence was not binding upon them; the
judge's charge was not binding; nothing was. The law did not
concern itself with the question of how they reached their verdict. This curiously irrational element in the jury system

proved, of course, to be a great protection to accused persons in many cases, whatever their actual guilt. If a jury, moved by whim, mercy, sympathy, or pigheadedness, refused to convict against all law and evidence, the prisoner was freed, and that was that. The doctrine as James Bradley Thayer said, was "ancient that one should not be twice put in jeopardy of life or limb for the same offense." On the other hand, a trial jury prejudiced against a defendant might return a verdict of guilty, but the judge, if convinced of unfairness in such a case, could reprieve the prisoner and recommend that the king pardon him.

The finality of the jury's verdict of not guilty, in a criminal case, probably derived from the fact that the jury originated when the older forms of proof—compurgation, ordeal, and battle—had not yet died out. The verdict of the inquest took on the same conclusiveness as any judgment of God, especially because the jurors were originally witnesses whose oaths were decisive. By the late fourteenth century the requirement of a unanimous verdict became settled practice, adding to the authority of verdicts. In a 1367 case a court ruled that a verdict reached by eleven of twelve jurors was unacceptable. The rule of unanimity may have originated, as Pollock and Maitland said, because the test was the voice of the country and the country supposedly could have but one voice. The origin of the rule may also be found in the fact that, in early trials by witnesses and compurgators, there was a requirement of unanimity. If one compurgator failed to make the oath by just the right formula or perjured himself, the oath "burst." By the same analogy, the failure of a jury to agree "burst" the verdict. A unanimous verdict by the inquest, which was regarded as representative of the country, an expression of its sense, carried a supernatural weight. In any case, the sworn inquest, having succeeded the older forms of proof, inherited many of their characteristics, including that of finality.

In civil cases, but never in the instance of a criminal verdict, when jurors were still regarded as witnesses the court considered a false verdict as a form of perjury, punishable by a special process known as the "attaint." A special jury of twenty-four tried the civil jury that gave the false verdict, and its members, if convicted, could be punished severely. As jurors lost their character as witnesses, the attaint fell into disuse; by the sixteenth century it was rarely employed and then only rarely successful. Juries in criminal cases, though never subject to the attaint, could be threatened with punishment by the Star Chamber for a false verdict, but the threat was more often than not an idle one calculated to intimidate rather than force a verdict of guilty. In the first half of the sixteenth century, almost every term of the Star Chamber saw some grand inquest or jury fined for acquitting felons or murderers, but that practice also died. One of the last examples of its use occurred after the trial of Sir Nicholas Throckmorton in 1554.

Throckmorton was tried by a jury for high treason because of his complicity in Wyatt's Rebellion, which grew out of opposition to the marriage of Queen Mary to Philip of Spain. A treason trial, above all others, most directly involved the security of the state, and even a common-law court of that period would conduct the trial in the interests of the sovereign, determined on a conviction. But only the jury could convict, and it might acquit. Throckmorton had been imprisoned for fifty-eight days preceding the day of the trial; he had had no opportunity to prepare his case and had been kept in ignorance of the evidence against him. He had to defend himself, and do it extemporaneously; counsel was not permitted in such cases until 1695. He heard the indictment read against him but had no copy of it. Not till 1696 did defendants in treason cases have a right to a copy of the indictment. He had no right to call witnesses on his behalf either; when he saw in the courtroom a man whom he wanted to give testimony for him, the chief justice ordered the man out. With only the slimmest opportunity for making an effective defense, Throckmorton nevertheless had the very great advantage of being tried publicly before a jury and the freedom to say whatever he wished, and he made the most of it. Defending himself with astonishing vigor and agility, he engaged in a spirited altercation with the crown's counsel and even with the chief justice on points of law as well as fact. He was allowed the liberty of correcting the court's summation to the jury and of making a speech to the jury following the summation. He won an acquittal. The jury's verdict certainly proved the comparative fairness of even an imperfect accusatorial procedure.

The jurors, however, were punished for their audacity. The court, unable to touch Throckmorton, imprisoned all twelve jurors. Four who "made their submission, and owned their offense" were freed, but the remaining eight, after six months in jail, were heavily fined by the Star Chamber and then were discharged. Sir Thomas Smith, about a decade later, observed that if a jury "having pregnant evidence" acquitted a defendant, "which they will do sometime," he went free, but the judge rebuked the jurors and threatened them with punishment. "But this threatening chanceth oftener than the execution thereof, and the twelve answer with most gentle words they did it according to their consciences and . . . as they thought right and . . . so it passeth away for the most part." Alluding to Throckmorton's case, he noted the punishment of the jury, yet added, "But these doings were even then by many accounted very violent, tyrannical, and contrary to the liberty and custom of the realm of England. Wherefore it cometh very seldom in use."

Thus, although the rule was not finally established until Edward Bushell's case in 1670 that a jury could not be punished for having acquitted a defendant against the evidence or the direction of the court, juries were free to render verdicts of their choice, with impunity, after Throckmorton's case. Notwithstanding their sometimes erratic and even inexplicable behavior, their tendency to reflect public prejudice, and their capability of being intimidated by the court, trial juries were England's major barrier against the growth of the inquisitional mode of procedure.

In sum, then, criminal procedure on the Continent, in both ecclesiastical and secular courts was thoroughly inquisitorial while England's procedure remained essentially accusatorial. The two systems originated in the same source, the inquest, and developed at the same time but in divergent directions. In one there was no definite accuser, lest it be the judge himself whose suspicions were aroused by common report or secret information; in the other there was a definite accuser whose charges against a person led to his preliminary examination by a justice of the peace. The inquisitorial system did not provide for a specification and revelation of the charges; the accusatorial system, utilizing the grand jury to screen the charges, provided them in a detailed indictment. The inquisitorial system surrounded every step in the proceedings with secrecy, making unchecked tyranny inevitable; the accusatorial system was substantially public. The former was nonconfrontative, revealing not even the names of the witnesses against the accused; the latter was essentially confrontative, naming the witnesses, producing their depositions in court, and with some exceptions in treason trials allowing them to give sworn testimony before the accused and the jury.

One system presumed the guilt of the accused; the other, requiring the prosecution to prove its case to a jury, did not. The one forced the accused to submit to a self-incriminatory oath; the other did not even permit the accused to give sworn testimony if he wanted to. One tried the accused by secret interrogatories, the other by public evidence. One was an official prosecution by the judge; the other made the trial an oral combat before a jury of the accused's peers, with the public watching, the crown's attorney prosecuting, and the judge basically passive. One empowered the judge to decide the question of guilt or innocence, while the other permitted a jury to control the verdict. One routinely used torture; the other regarded it as illegal. One utilized a stringent and sophisticated law of evidence, the theory of "legal proofs," while the other was almost casual about the nature of evidence. One made an absolute differentiation between civil and criminal procedure; the other employed essentially the same litigious procedure for both.

One, not recognizing the concept of double jeopardy, retried a suspect indefinitely, while the other would place no one in jeopardy more than once for the same offense in a capital case, and every felony was a capital crime. Finally, one was cruel and arbitrary; the other was potentially fair and just, especially because a jury's verdict controlled the outcome.

What accounts for England's singular escape from the fate of the continental nations of Europe? The most likely answer is that the accusatorial system of procedure, with a comparatively neutral judge presiding and a jury deciding the outcome, effectively served the needs of the state, thus making unnecessary the employment of the inquisitorial system. Fortuitous timing seems to have made a great difference, too. Pollock and Maitland wrote that England had a narrow escape. The old forms of proof were breaking down. "Happily, however, the reforms of Henry II were effected before the days of Innocent III." Just how narrow was the escape is shown by the fact that Henry II died in 1189, only nine years before Innocent III became pope. But the great Angevin's reforms were instituted in the 1160s and 1170s. In something of overstatement, Pollock and Maitland remarked that "the whole of English law is centralized and unified" by the establishment of royal judges, their frequent eyres throughout the land, and "by the introduction of the 'inquest' or 'recognition' and the 'original writ' as normal parts of the machinery of justice."

Not only was English law centralized early; the English state itself was centralized earlier than that of any other country, and one of the foremost means of achieving that centralization was the system of royal justice employing the inquest, which became both the grand jury and the petty jury. Sir William Holdsworth best made the point: "Thus it happened that the delegates of royal power could make their influence felt all over the country, and royal justice everywhere superseded the justice administered by the local courts. One of the most important instruments of the royal power was the inquisition held under the supervision of a royal judge by means of a jury. And, wherever the royal justice was introduced, this method of determining facts accompanied it. Thus the jury system spread as rapidly and as widely as the justice of the royal courts, and as the rules of that common-law which those courts were both making and administering. But the rapidity of the development of the common-law caused it to produce a set of fixed principles before the ideals of the civil and canon lawyers had time to exercise an overwhelming influence upon the substance of its rules."

Thus English rules of criminal law retained many archaic ideas, keeping the new jury procedure as accusatorial as the older modes of proof. The jury system was a new mode of proof, or at least was treated as if it were a mode of proof. It was therefore based on consent, and its results were taken as final. The judges took the path of least resistance by accepting verdicts rather than by making their own inquiries, a step that would have led to an inquisitorial system. The unsophisticated state of the law of evidence, which was indeed in its rudimentary stages, made it additionally easy for the judges to accept the findings of a band of witnesses, the sworn inquest. Not the least result was that the English judge, relieved of the necessity of making his own determination of guilt or innocence, gained enhanced dignity and impartiality. These wholesome benefits would have been impossible had the crown not been able to adapt the accusatorial system of justice to the needs of the state. The sworn inquest, however, did serve to augment the exchequer, control local feudatories, and enforce the king's peace. By contrast the French monarchy, a century after Henry II centralized England, had extended royal jurisdiction over the royal domain only. The inquisitorial system became a powerful instrument for centralizing France, as the accusatorial had in England.

England was also less susceptible to the influences of the canon and civil lawyers of the Continent because of its isolation. For the same reason, perhaps, the contagion of heresy scarcely infected England; her orthodoxy in religion until the late fourteenth century was also a settling force, a bulwark against the need for ecclesiastical inquisitions. When heresy became widespread in England, the accusatorial system was well established, and nationalism, anti-clericalism, and the weakness of the papacy prevented a papal inquisition. For these reasons trial by jury developed and flourished in England. The institution of the jury enlisted popular support on the side of the common-law courts. Trial by jury became a form of democratic involvement in the administration of criminal justice.

CHAPTER III

❧

The Double Jury System

IN 1998 a public opinion poll revealed that most Americans eligible to serve on a jury asserted that they would act on their own beliefs as to right and wrong, regardless of a judge's instructions on the law of a case. Had a similar poll been taken three and a half centuries earlier, the results would have been the same. Jury verdicts then and now reflected jury opinions.

In 1623 Ferdinando Pulton published a treatise on "Triall by the Countrie," in which he declared that the jury system was founded on the thirty-ninth section of Magna Carta. That proposition was historically inaccurate but became the universal and profound belief of all Englishmen. Lord Chief Justice Edward Coke, in his commentary on Magna Carta, endorsed that view and praised trial by jury, "indictment or presentment of good, and lawful men, where such deeds be done," and common-law procedures.

In 1649 the irrepressibly cantankerous democrat and Leveller leader, John Lilburne, was tried by a jury before an extraordinary panel of magistrates including eight common-law judges, the lord mayor of London, the recorder of London, four sergeants-at-law, and twenty-six other special judges including city aldermen and members of Parliament. Lilburne dazzled the great audience with his declamations on the rights of an accused person to the fundamentals of fair play from the time of arrest through trial. He appealed to the jury over the heads of his judges, depicting the court as his oppressors, and his jurors as his protectors. It was a political trial, and Lilburne conducted himself as if public opinion on affairs of state and matters of liberty and justice would be decisive. Against the authority of the judges, he openly appealed to the jury, telling them that they were the judges of law as well as of fact. The court, indignantly rejecting his aspersions on its authority, denied that the jury could decide matters of law, but Lilburne persisted in reading from Sir Edward Coke's works to teach the jury the law governing his case. The court could not shut him up. He called upon the jury to witness the fact that the court refused him free speech to conduct his defense. Finally getting his way, he expounded law to the jury. The jury acquitted him, despite the court's rulings.

When he was again tried for his life in 1653, a jury once more acquitted him in the face of Cromwell's bullying tactics. Parliament ordered the examination of the jury before the Council of State. The foreman would say only that he had acted in accordance with his conscience; he would answer no questions. Another juror, when asked to account for his verdict, replied that he refused to incriminate himself but finally declared that he did not think the court had the right to try Lilburne. Asked why, he replied that he was accountable only to

God and would not otherwise answer. Another juror admitted that despite the rulings of the court, "He and the rest of the jury took themselves to be Judges of matter of law, as well as matter of fact"—proof that Lilburne had persuaded them. Cromwell was able to best Lilburne only by acting against the law.

In 1670 in London, William Penn and William Mead were criminally prosecuted because they sought to practice their Quaker convictions. Technically the charge was disturbance of the peace. A generation earlier the first Quakers did in fact disturb the peace and the quiet worship of the other Christians whom the Quakers at that time regarded as Antichrists. But by 1670 the Quakers had become law-abiding quietists who wanted only to be let alone and no longer disrupted the religious services of others. Nevertheless Anglicans, who returned to power as the established Church of England after the demise of the Cromwells, remembered Quakers with considerable hostility. Parliamentary legislation, dictated by Anglicans, inflicted fines and imprisonment on the supposedly dangerous opinions and practices of Quakers. Only Anglican worship was lawful until the Toleration Act of 1689. Accordingly, when Quakers who had been dispossessed from their meeting houses congregated in public places to conduct peaceable worship, they were apprehended, jailed, and prosecuted.

Penn was twenty-six in 1670 and had been a member of the Society of Friends for three years. As one who did not attend the services of the Church of England, he was bound to get into trouble. Any religious leader who did not receive Anglican ordination, follow Anglican rites, and use the Anglican prayer book would necessarily violate the Conventicles Act of 1664, which outlawed any religious services other than Anglican. The act's objective was to suppress the growing and dangerous practices of "seditious sectaries and other disloyal persons" who met under "pretense of conscience" to "contrive insurrections." Quakers suffered disproportionately among non-conformists because they felt obligated to condemn the Conventicles Act, to deny the payment of fines, and to refuse to give sureties for what the courts called "good behavior." Such behavior, in the Quakers' view, would have required them to become apostates, converts to Anglicanism. Thus of the tens of thousands of nonconformists who suffered for conscience's sake after the 1660 restoration of the Stuarts, Quakers easily constituted the most numerous sect.

Penn and Mead, whom the authorities regarded as seditious sectaries, spent most of 1669 in the Tower of London. When released, the dictates of their faith required them to challenge the government. They sought to assemble and pray in their meeting house, only to be dispossessed by force. Penn and Mead then attempted to hold their meeting in a public street and were rearrested. The charge against them was that they had assembled at the head of a so-called "mob" of at least three hundred people and tumultuously preached in contempt of the crown and to the disturbance of the peace.

At their trial, Penn and Mead pleaded not guilty but were at once cited for contempt and fined forty marks because they refused in Quaker fashion to remove their hats in court. When their jurors had been sworn in, the lieutenant of the Tower objected to one Edward Bushell, who failed to kiss the Anglican

Book of Common Prayer. But the court allowed him to take his seat as a juror. The court of ten judges verbally harassed the defendants and demanded a verdict of guilty from the jury if the jury acknowledged that the Quakers had met at all, as in fact they had.

Mead, when asked whether he had been present at the outlawed meeting, invoked his right against self-incrimination. Penn also refused to cooperate, claiming that he was being tried merely because he worshiped God. The court reprimanded him for failing to acknowledge that his violations of the law caused the proceedings against him. Nevertheless, he informed the jury that the indictment had no foundation in law. One of the royal judges then called Penn "a pestilent fellow," threatened to gag him so that he could not speak, and ordered both prisoners to be kept in the bale-dock during the trial. The bale-dock, which Penn called a "stinking hole," was a sort of holding cell. Penn, appealing to his jurors, demanded his rights as an Englishman, and Mead, also addressing the jurors, told them that they were his only judges; he lectured them on what constituted a riot. A judge observed that he ought to have his tongue cut out. From the bale-dock, Penn, in a loud voice, notified the jurors that the judges were violating his rights under Magna Carta, but a judge informed the jurors that the guilt of the prisoners had been proved.

When four of the twelve jurors voted to acquit Mead, the court blamed one of them, Bushell, for having influenced the others contrary to the court's instructions. Bushell was told that he deserved to be indicted for his impudence, and the jurors were again instructed to fulfill their obligations. When asked for their verdict, the foreman of the jury declared, "Guilty of speaking in Gracechurch Street." One judge remarked they might as well have said nothing, and another asked whether they meant guilty of an unlawful assembly. Bushell and the other minority jurors stood by their verdict. That spurred a judge to vilify them "with the most opprobrious language." Another judge told the jurors that they could not depart until they announced a verdict, provoking the recalcitrant jurors to insist that they had already given a verdict of not guilty.

The next morning, when the court again demanded to know whether the jury had reached a verdict, the foreman repeated its decision: "Guilty of speaking in Gracechurch Street." The court inquired, "To an unlawful assembly?" Bushell denied it. When the court threatened to starve the jurors until they returned a "positive verdict," Penn inquired whether the court accepted the verdict in Mead's case. The judges replied that no verdict existed. They reasoned that the two men had been indicted for conspiracy, and because one had been found not guilty and the other had received no verdict, "it could not be a verdict." Penn nevertheless explained that the jury having acquitted Mead, he, Penn, was also free because "you have indicted us for a conspiracy, and I could not possibly conspire alone." The jury again repeated its verdict of guilty of speaking in the street, spurring the court to threaten that it would order the slitting of Bushell's nose. Penn angrily retorted that justice was impossible when juries were threatened and their verdicts rejected. A judge urged that Penn be gagged, tied, and staked to the ground, adding that instituting the Spanish Inquisition in England might be beneficial.

Despite judicial recriminations against the jury, the jurors remained unbudgeable. The next day, when again asked for a verdict, they repeated their previous finding until the court so exasperated them that they reversed themselves by declaring that Penn was "not guilty." The court promptly fined each juror forty marks and ordered them all imprisoned until they paid the fines. When Penn insisted that he should be set free in accord with the jury's verdict, the court replied that he must be incarcerated in Newgate Prison along with his jurors until all fines were paid. The jurors were later discharged by the Court of Common Pleas, which ruled that their commitment was illegal.

Bushell, however, had sought a writ of habeas corpus, thereby earning special attention from the King's Bench, the highest criminal court. Vaughn, the lord chief justice of England, delivered its opinion freeing him. Observing that Bushell's jailer was obligated to declare in his return to the writ the reasons for imprisonment, Vaughn insisted that the jailer must be as specific as possible. But the return in this case was so general, he explained, that the cause of Bushell's imprisonment could not be ascertained. Allowing a court to imprison a juror for contempt on the ground that he had voted for an acquittal against the court's instructions on the law of the case subverted the functions of the jury. Indeed, the jury became a useless institution, Vaughn reasoned, if the judge controlled its understanding of the meaning of the law, which it was obligated to decide for itself. The jury could discharge its functions, said Vaughn, only if it was exempt from the judge's power to fine and jail its members. By such reasoning, the King's Bench emancipated juries, allowing them ever after to return verdicts based on their grasp of the law as well as of the facts. Thus in 1697 Lord Chief Justice Holt reaffirmed that "in all cases and in all actions the jury may give a general or a special verdict, as well in causes criminal as civil, and the Court ought to receive it." The king could dismiss judges and discipline lawyers, but jurors were impregnable.

Regardless of the faults of the criminal justice system, the prisoner in a criminal case knew the charges against him, confronted his accusers, and had the freedom to give to the jury his own explanations. Furthermore, he could question and argue with the prosecution's witnesses in the presence of the jury sitting in judgment of him. Criminal defendants suffered from many disadvantages—lack of counsel, lack of witnesses on their own behalf, lack of time to prepare their defense—yet the public trial before a jury was supremely fair judged by any standard known in the eighteenth-century world. Sir William Blackstone summed it up when he wrote:

> But in settling and adjusting a question of fact, when entrusted to any single magistrate, partiality and injustice had an ample field to range in; either by asserting that to be proved which is not so, or by more artfully suppressing some circumstances, stretching and varying others, and distinguishing away the remainder. Here, therefore, a competent number of sensible and upright jurymen, chosen by lot from among those of the middle rank, will be found the best investigators of truth, and the surest guardians of public justice. For the most powerful individuals in the

state will be cautious of committing any flagrant invasion of another's right, when he knows that the fact of his oppression may be examined and decided by twelve indifferent men, not appointed until the hour of the trial; and that, when once the fact is ascertained, the law must of course redress it. This, therefore, preserves in the hands of the people that share which they ought to have in the administration of general justice, and prevents the encroachments of the powerful and wealthy citizens.

Notwithstanding Blackstone's praise for the objectivity of juries, trial by jury was equivalent to trial by the local community, and trial by the local community could be trial by local prejudice. Moreover, jurors could be improperly influenced in a variety of ways. Some early juries reached results not in accord with facts, probably because of prejudiced direction from the bench or threats from partisans of one of the parties. A wrong verdict could result in punishment of the jurors. They could be fined, imprisoned, and subjected to forfeiture of property for verdicts proved to be wrong. They could also be punished when judges, appointees of the crown and still its lackeys, disagreed with a verdict that conflicted with the crown's wishes. As the "surest guardians of public justice," juries deserved their reputation for also guarding personal liberties, and grand juries enjoyed a similar reputation.

The grand jury, like the trial jury, did in fact evolve into a bastion of popular rights rather than into a crown agent. When refusing to indict, grand juries protected individuals whom prosecutors would have liked to put to trial without a well-founded accusation. Eventually the theory developed that no one should be indicted without a *prima facie* case of guilt— enough evidence to convict if standing by itself, unrebutted. Sir John Hawles, in his tract *The Englishmen's Rights* (1680), championed grand juries as defenders of individual freedom because they protected against unfounded or spiteful prosecution. Further, Hawles argued that no courts or government agencies could punish grand juries by fines or imprisonment. The refusal of a grand jury in 1681 to indict Lord Shaftesbury for treason, despite the urgings of Charles II, enhanced Englishmen's respect for the grand jury as an institution that shielded them from vindictive or malicious motives of the state; Shaftesbury, however, fled the country to avoid an indictment by a more compliant grand jury in another county.

Sir John Somers, the lord chancellor of England, declared in his aptly titled tract of 1682, *The Security of Englishmen's Lives*, "Grand juries are our only security, in as much as our lives cannot be drawn into jeopardy by all the malicious crafts of the devil, unless such a number of our honest countrymen shall be satisfied in the truth of the accusations." Henry Care's *English Liberties or Free Born Subject's Inheritance* (1698) vigorously repeated the same point. Grand jurors did more than interpose between the king's prosecutor and the trial jury; they also acted as representatives of their locality by denouncing governmental abuses, recommending new laws, and even administering statutory law. Blackstone's *Commentaries on the Laws of England* explained that grand juries stood between the liberties of the people and the prerogatives of the crown, thus permitting the grand jury to thwart executive impulses to imprison politically obnoxious subjects or to exile them.

In the American colonies, where grand juries were chosen by law-enforcement officers such as sheriffs or constables, or by county court judges, the jurors were usually large freeholders or prosperous townsfolk. In most of the colonies, prosecutors tried criminal cases that had first involved an accusation by a grand jury. Hawles's *Englishmen's Rights*, Somers's *Security of Englishmen's Lives*, and Care's *English Liberties* were each reprinted at least twice in America and circulated throughout the colonies, serving as manuals on the functions and authority of grand juries. These books taught that grand juries defended personal liberty. Had a grand jury been able to prevail in New York in 1734–1735, John Peter Zenger would never have been tried for seditiously libeling the provincial governor. Two different grand juries refused to indict him, forcing the crown prosecutor to proceed by independently filing in court an accusation against him known as an "information." The prosecutor filed the information by himself, that is, made the decision without grand jury endorsement to prosecute.

The earliest American grand juries met in the towns of Massachusetts in accordance with an act of the provincial legislature ordering town meetings to select grand jurors periodically. These early grand juries presented scores and scores of suspected offenders, including even some of the magistrates of Massachusetts. Town meetings elected the jurors who, after 1641, were obligated to serve for one year. They were free to investigate any abuses of government powers and any laxity in town governance. Thus grand jurors reproved towns for neglecting to repair bridges and roads, for questionable land sales, and for other failures to serve the public properly. Additionally, grand juries presented individuals for abuses such as giving short weight when selling commodities, not properly grinding grain, violating the Sabbath, getting intoxicated in public, or using foul language.

Connecticut was responsible for an innovation that eventually became influential. Instead of leaving presentments to town meetings, Connecticut relied on local prosecutors to file an information before a court. In most colonies, however, county courts rather than town meetings selected the grand jurors who brought the accusation in serious cases; in some colonies, sheriffs selected panels of prosperous freeholders; in still others, justices of the peace named the grand jurors. Usually grand juries attended the county courts, but their functions remained diverse. They not only brought accusations of crime; they also undertook a variety of investigations on behalf of county courts and even administered various laws. Practice varied, of course, in each colony. In the Jerseys, grand juries assisted county courts in levying county taxes. In Pennsylvania, grand juries inspected public works such as courthouses, jails, and roads in order to determine whether any official had been neglectful in their construction. In Georgia, grand juries reflected a variety of complaints on behalf of the public against the government.

Grand juries also became a favorite instrument for Americans to express their protests against British policies. Grand juries were able to protect Americans in some colonies because of provincial statutes that banned prosecutions except upon a presentment originating with a grand jury. Previously, crown prosecutors had been able to decide for themselves who should be put to trial by merely filing an information. Americans would not have been able to challenge royal powers as effectively as they did if grand juries had not stood between royal prosecutors and trial by jury. American grand jurors, for example, refused to indict rioters who in 1765 destroyed the tax stamps in Boston, and three years later grand jurors failed to indict newspaper editors who libeled the royal governor of Massachusetts. Indeed, for fear of retaliation, no one would testify on behalf of British interests before a grand jury in cases involving recent British policies affecting the American colonies. As a result, those policies failed at the enforcement level, leaving crown officials impotent.

In Massachusetts, grand juries were a patriotic American instrument for harassing tactics that aimed to stymie British policies. Consequently Britain sought to evade grand juries. Lord North, the British leader, persuaded the House of Commons to change the charter of Massachusetts by preventing town meetings except when called by the royal governor. Moreover, the House of Commons authorized Massachusetts sheriffs to appoint all jurors. Previously the people in their town meeting had elected grand jurors whenever they were needed. Lord North censured grand juries for opposing British measures. In turn, the people of Massachusetts vehemently denounced Britain and in circular letters to other colonies declared that the appointment of grand jurors by sheriffs constituted tyranny. Throughout Massachusetts, town meetings, which repudiated the new system as subversive of justice, encouraged law-enforcement officers to ignore the new law. The towns persisted in holding their meetings at which those in attendance elected grand jurors. Sheriffs who complied with British law were coerced into reconsidering their fealty to royal policies.

Grand jurors in most colonies defied royally appointed judges who had encouraged them to indict their neighbors for having illegally opposed Britain. In several colonies grand juries issued public statements intended as propaganda for the patriot cause, and some patriot judges indulged in equally offensive charges to grand and petty juries alike. In Philadelphia a grand jury denounced the payments and salaries of royal officials from revenues collected from the tea tax; the grand jury even advocated a boycott against English products. Grand juries commonly advocated intercolonial actions to redress grievances against Britain. Like trial juries, the grand juries of the Revolutionary era, claiming the rights of Englishmen, curbed the enforcement of objectionable acts by government officials. Grand juries promoted American resistance and generally served as popular spokesmen. Even during the War for Independence, grand juries continued their multiple functions. They governed their localities as well as presented offenders. They investigated not only law enforcement but also the physical conditions of roads, bridges, and ferries; they supervised the prices of commodities; and they fixed the rates of taxes, audited public records, and generally compelled local governing bodies to meet regularly and to be more responsive to public needs.

CHAPTER IV

🍁

Trial Juries

FROM THE EARLIEST POSSIBLE DATE, English colonists in the American wilderness employed trial by jury in criminal cases. Royal instructions of 1606 for the governance of Virginia provided that offenders be tried by a jury before the governor and council. Moreover, the Virginia charter of 1606 contained a provision, repeated in later charters of Virginia and in the charters of virtually all other colonies, guaranteeing colonists the rights of Englishmen as if they still resided in the mother country. Trial juries in Virginia had a right to decide questions of law, and Thomas Jefferson in his *Notes on Virginia* observed that although colonial judges had instructed juries on the law of a case, often the law and facts were so closely related that the best policy was for juries to decide the law as well as the facts. The reason, he explained, was that "the common sense of twelve honest men" enhanced the chances of a "just decision."

The Plymouth colony guaranteed trial by jury for accused persons, and in Massachusetts, shortly after courts began to operate, they worked with trial juries, though in petty cases magistrates sitting without juries settled cases. In 1630 the officers of the province appointed from their ranks several who were vested with the power of English justices of the peace. They could try offenders without juries and punish them in cases of misdemeanor. In 1643 the provincial legislature declared that only its verdict or that of a jury could banish an offender or authorize his execution. Thomas Lechford, an English lawyer who lived for a time in Massachusetts, observed in 1638 that juries tried a variety of matters, including trespass, heresy, and debts. He noted too that in jury trials, matters of law and fact were not distinguished; juries decided both. The right to trial by jury received formal recognition in the Massachusetts Body of Liberties of 1641, which authorized parties in civil suits, as well as persons accused of crime, to choose whether to be tried by judges or by a jury, and also authorized challenges to jurors for cause. Practice in Connecticut and Rhode Island was similar, and in New York, as soon as the English took control, all cases were tried by juries, although juries of six or seven were common for petty offenses.

By 1642 capital punishment could be inflicted in Massachusetts only after a jury's verdict of guilty. So too in Rhode Island. Women, Negroes, and servants could not serve as jurors. Sheriffs summoned jurors from among white property-owning men, mainly bystanders, who were rarely challenged for cause. A statute of 1647 authorized magistrates to decide petty cases, but any person who was convicted had a right to appeal to a higher court sitting with a jury. Jury trial was infrequent, however, because the party requesting it was obligated to pay jurors and costs. Jurors received about three shillings daily. In an unusual jury trial of 1677 in Ipswich, Massachusetts, involving a dispute between a preacher and his congregation, the preacher, Jeremiah Shepard, brought suit to obtain his overdue stipend; the jury awarded him fifty pounds.

Juries might sometimes return special verdicts in contrast to a general verdict of guilty or not guilty. A special verdict indicated only the jury's finding of the facts, leaving to the court a decision of which party should win. Runaway juries, however, might breach the agreement of both parties to be governed by a special verdict. John Adams observed that if a jury believed it knew the law, it had no obligation to find a special verdict. In a Maryland case of 1714, for example, the parties agreed to abide by a special verdict and the court instructed the jury to return such a verdict, but this jury returned a general verdict for one party. Despite the other's objection, the court held that the jury was free to decide as it wished. In other cases, juries found general verdicts after the parties had agreed to accept a special verdict. The short of it is that no way existed to keep a jury leashed except to bypass it altogether in minor cases that could be decided summarily by a magistrate.

Summary jurisdiction by magistrates was normal for petty offenses and remains normal even today. The Constitution, in Article III, stipulates that the "trial of *all* crimes" [my italics], excepting cases of impeachment, shall be by jury, and the Sixth Amendment reinforces that by asserting that "in *all* criminal prosecutions, the accused shall enjoy the right to a speedy and public trial, by an impartial jury" of the vicinage. But juries did not and do not judge all crimes or all criminal prosecutions if offenders have committed misdemeanors. In England, justices of the peace, sitting without juries, decided all offenses less than felonies. Parliamentary legislation persistently authorized magistrates alone to settle petty infractions of the law. When Richard Burns, himself a justice of the peace, wrote his widely used manual on the subject, he enumerated a couple of hundred offenses that the crown could prosecute before a magistrate without a jury. Vagrancy, assaults, drunkenness, swearing, disorderly conduct, smuggling, and violations of liquor laws and Sabbath laws were among them.

In 1768 Matthew Bacon's *Abridgment of the Laws* said of the exclusive power of magistrates over inferior offenses: "The Jurisdiction herein given to Justices of the Peace by particular statutes is so various, and extends to such a Multiplicity of Cases, that it were endless to endeavor to enumerate them," and Blackstone made a similar comment. Richard Burns's *Justice of the Peace*, first published in 1755 and frequently reprinted in England and America, made this striking remark: "The power of a justice of the peace is in restraint of the common law, and in abundance of instances is a tacit repeal of that famous clause in the great charter, that a man shall be tried by his equals." Because the magistrate's summary jurisdiction was so speedy and cheap, it drastically limited the right of trial by jury.

In America all the colonies utilized summary jurisdiction over minor offenses, despite professions of allegiance to trial by jury. Justices of the peace in all the colonies, working without juries, rendered judgment in cases of lesser crimes such as swearing, breach of peace, vagrancy, profanity, violating the

Sabbath, drunkenness, breaking fences, and arming Indians. Juries everywhere, however, determined the outcome of accusations of serious crimes or felonies. If a jury could not reach a verdict, its members were free to consult with any person for advice. In some sparsely settled areas in America, six-member juries tried cases involving minor infractions such as trespass or drunkenness, or involving small amounts of money, usually less than ten pounds. Twelve was the usual number, however, for the jury's size. Nearly all colonial charters possessed a clause similar to that in the charter of West Jersey, which specified that unless convicted by a jury consisting of twelve men of the neighborhood, no one could lose life, liberty, or property in a civil or criminal case.

In Connecticut, New Hampshire, Rhode Island, and Vermont, colonial judges exercised circumscribed powers; they presided to ensure order and fairness, but juries decided all matters of law as well as fact. Colonial judges were usually laymen, not lawyers, and therefore were no more qualified than jurors. In Massachusetts the General Court (the legislature) intervened when a jury disagreed. If the two branches of the legislature also disagreed, the magistrates deferred to a jury verdict unless it clearly conflicted with the law or the evidence. Trial by jury was hailed in colonial Massachusetts as "the great liberty of an English subject."

In 1669 the celebrated Fundamental Constitutions for the Carolinas, framed by the great John Locke, fixed steep property qualifications for jurors and allowed them to decide cases by majority vote. South Carolina selected jurors in a unique manner: a child drew the names of jurors from a box containing the names of all eligible men. For decades, jurors met only in Charleston, where the sole court in the province sat.

In New York, as soon as the English superseded the Dutch in 1665, they instituted jury trials; in all but cases involving capital crimes, for which twelve-member juries were required, juries consisted of six or seven men. Jacob Leisler was tried capitally in 1691. The charge of treason derived from his rebellion against the royal governor, Henry Sloughter, who ordered his arrest. The jury convicted Leisler and his son-in-law, and they were subjected to the grisly punishment for treason. They were hanged, cut down when still alive, their sex organs were cut off, they were disemboweled, the excised body parts were burned before their eyes, they were beheaded and cut into quarters, and their heads were displayed on pikes. Convicting a person of treason was the most terrible fate a jury could inflict.

In 1674 one party to a civil suit in Massachusetts argued that juries as well as magistrates were judges of the law because they were sworn "to goe by Law." That was probably the first claim in America that juries decided law as well as facts. In 1676, when William Penn framed the Fundamental Laws of West New Jersey, he reaffirmed the famous clause of Magna Carta on judgment by one's peers and pledged that "without a due tryal, and judgment passed by twelve good and lawful men of the neighborhood," no person should be deprived of life, limb, liberty, or property. In 1683 the proprietors of East New Jersey did the same, adding that judges "shall pronounce such judgment as they shall receive from, and be directed by the said twelve men in whom only the judgment resides, and not otherwise." The proprietors also provided that all trials, civil and criminal, should be open to the public in both Jerseys.

William Penn's law for Pennsylvania also decreed public trials by twelve-member juries. Nevertheless, in 1692 when George Keith, the leader of a separatist faction among Pennsylvania Quakers, assailed the deputy governor and the magistrates, leading to his prosecution for seditious libel and disturbance of the peace, the magistrates whom he had assailed tried him summarily, without a jury. They convicted him and his associate, William Bradford. The two men escaped sentence by invoking Magna Carta and their right to trial by jury. The judges yielded. After several months in jail, Bradford, who was Pennsylvania's first printer, got his trial, but not before the prosecutor remarked that the jury's only task was to decide whether Bradford had printed the seditious tract. In reply Bradford contended that the jury had to try the whole of the matter, the criminality of the publication as well as his responsibility for it. After the allegation that the jury had merely to determine the authorship of the tract, the colloquy between Bradford and his prosecutors went as follows:

Bradford. "That is not only what they are to find, they are to find also, whether this be a seditious paper, or not, & whether it does tend to the weakening of the hands of the Magistrate."

Attorney. "No, this is a matter of Law, which the Jury is not to meddle with. But find whether W. B. printed it or not, and the Bench is to judge whether it be a seditious Paper or not; for the Law has determined what is a Breach of the Peace, and the penalty, which the Bench only is to give judgment on."

Judge Jennings. "You are only to try, whether W. B. printed it, or not."

Bradford. "That is wrong; for the Jury are Judges in Law, as well as in matter of Fact."

The court, of course, disagreed. The jury's verdict was inconclusive. Three of its members would have acquitted. There is a story, unverifiable, that Bradford was saved by a sympathetic juror who, while examining the typeform that was used to print the seditious tract, accidentally shoved the bottom of the form with his cane, whereupon it came apart and all the type collapsed to the floor, and with it the prosecution's case. Bradford was recommitted to prison where he remained another eight months before being released by a new governor.

The Pennsylvania Assembly in 1700 passed an act protecting freemen's privileges, reaffirming Magna Carta's celebrated Section 29 and associating it wrongly but significantly with an accused's right to trial by jury. From time to time similar legislation was reenacted in Pennsylvania.

Thomas Maule, an irascible Quaker merchant of Salem, Massachusetts, published a book in 1695 that was so aspersive a commentary on the civil and ecclesiastical rulers of the province that he was arrested for "Lyes and Slanders . . . upon the Government" as well as for doctrine that subverted "the true Christian religion." He was indicted by a grand jury and spent nearly a year in jail before he was finally tried. His prosecutor was the man who prevailed at the witchcraft trials. The court, backing the prosecutor, asked the jury to return a verdict of guilty because Maule's book tended to the overthrow of the Commonwealth and the church. Maule called on the jury to decide the law over the heads of judges, and the jury, to the court's dismay, returned a verdict of not guilty. The foreman, when asked to explain the verdict, declared that the jury believed that the prosecution should have been before ecclesiastical rather than civil figures and the verdict rendered by a "Jury of divines."

Nicholas Bayard and his friend John Hutchins were convicted of treason by a New York jury in 1702. Bayard was an influential politician who had addressed controversial letters to the king, Parliament, and the governor of New York. Hutchins, an alderman who used his tavern to solicit endorsements of Bayard's views, refused the order of Lieutenant Governor John Nanfan to turn over the documents. Nanfan imprisoned Hutchins and Bayard, charging them with treason. Following their conviction, they appealed to Queen Anne. Bayard stated that he had been convicted by an "illegal petty jury of Aliens and Dutch" who did not understand English laws or the English language. Two of his jurors acknowledged their ignorance and admitted that they did not know what high treason was; other jurors revealed their belief that the defendants should have been acquitted but voted guilty because of the foreman's influence. Hutchins, like Bayard, demanded to be retried by a jury of Englishmen. The presiding judge refused their requests, but the queen's ministers overturned the convictions. Bayard then attempted to have his judges arrested for misconduct, but they pleaded that an impartial jury had been responsible for the guilty verdicts. The jurors, in turn, refused to answer any questions, asserting that they had no obligation to do so. Thus the jury's verdict was undone but the jury remained independent.

Virginia, the mother dominion, was the site of an unusual witchcraft trial in 1706. A man and his wife accused a woman named Grace Sherwood of being a witch. The court ordered the sheriff to summon a jury of twelve matrons to try her. They returned a peculiar verdict after examining her, saying that they "found Two things like titts with several Spotts" on her body. The prosecutor, not knowing what to make of such a verdict, demanded that the female jurors try Sherwood again, but they made themselves scarce. Finally the court, with Sherwood's consent, decided to try her not by jury but by the old ordeal of water. Seated in a ducking stool, she was ducked in deep water. A good swimmer, she emerged safely, and the women jurors examined her again, but they failed or refused to return a verdict. The sheriff jailed her until she could be retried, but it seems that all charges against her were dropped, ending the case.

Beginning in 1720 John Trenchard and Thomas Gordon riveted the attention of Londoners with the publication of their essays on civil and religious liberty, *Cato's Letters*. That work, which was more esteemed and popular in the American colonies than John Locke's, hailed trial by jury as a cherished English right, but like virtually every other source on the subject was ritualist rather than analytical.

In 1723 James Franklin of Boston, Benjamin's older brother, who published the *New England Courant*, satirized the legislature, which ordered his arrest for affronting the government. Franklin felt incensed because the legislature had condemned him without affording him a fair trial by jury. He wrote a scathing denunciation of his treatment, invoking

Magna Carta and the rights of Englishmen, and complained that he had been denied the judgment of his peers. He then disregarded an order never again to print anything without first submitting it for approval to the secretary of the province. Franklin went into hiding to escape officers with a warrant for his arrest, first turning the paper over to brother Benjamin. When officers captured James, the government sought an indictment from a grand jury, but the jurors refused to indict him, thus protecting freedom of the press and fair trial.

The next notable case involved John Checkley, an Anglican minister, who published a book in 1724 reflecting on the Massachusetts government. He was tried for seditious words, but the jury, declining a verdict of guilty, returned a special verdict. The jurors found only that he had published the book. The court had to determine that it constituted seditious libel.

The celebrated 1735 case of John Peter Zenger originated in a power struggle between New York's royal governor, William Cosby, and a legislative faction determined to thwart his powers. That faction established a newspaper, published by Zenger, to compete with the one that supported the governor. Twice the governor failed to persuade a grand jury to indict Zenger and was forced to resort to an information, the accusatory device by which the government could initiate prosecutions independently. The charge against Zenger was seditious libel. At his trial, following nine months in prison, his counsel, Andrew Hamilton, admitted Zenger's responsibility for having printed the libelous articles, but argued that Zenger had a right to publish the truth concerning the governor.

The prosecutor, accurately reflecting the law, declared that because Zenger had admitted the publications, "the jury must find a verdict for the King, for supposing they were true . . . the law says their being true is an aggravation of the crime." Nevertheless, Hamilton, in an effort to turn the jury against the governor, offered to prove that the supposed libels were true, and he scored the doctrine that truth aggravated a libel. Were the jurors supposed to believe that "truth is a greater sin than falsehood"? When a matter of law was complicated by a matter of fact, he contended, "the jury have a right to determine both." If the jurors believed the truth of the alleged libels, they must free Zenger because, Hamilton argued, the law prohibited only false criticism. Appealing directly to the jury as a means of circumventing the royal judges, he stated, "Then, gentlemen of the jury, it is to you we must now appeal for witnesses to the truth of the facts."

Hamilton reminded the jurors that as citizens of New York they knew the facts concerning the supposed libels about the governor's administration. Contradicting the judges who had declared that the court alone decided whether the defendant's language violated the law, Hamilton advised the jurors that they, not the court, were the real judges; if they did not believe the words to be false, the publications were not criminal. "Jurymen are to see with their own eyes, to hear with their own ears, and to make use of their own consciences and understandings, in judging the lives, liberties or estates of their fellow subjects."

Chief Justice James DeLancey ruled that the jury's only task was to decide whether Zenger published the articles, leaving to the court a determination whether as a matter of law they were libelous. Hamilton responded that the court's rule "renders juries useless." He invoked the precedent of Bushell's case, in which the jury had decided against the rule of law laid down by the judges. The proper rule, according to Hamilton, was that the jury decided not just the fact of the publication but the question whether the words used were criminal. If the jury believed that Zenger had published the truth, the jury should acquit. Thus Hamilton used the jury as a court of public opinion, because the law was against Zenger. The jury voted not guilty, a victory for freedom of the press and the jury's power to make truth a defense against a charge of libel. It was also a triumph for the jury's authority to render a general verdict rather than just a special one limited to the question of whether a defendant in fact published the disputed words.

A spate of jury trials occurred in New York City in 1741 following the so-called "Negro Plot." The city's Negro population was the most numerous outside the South; about one-sixth of city folk were black. A sixteen-year-old indentured servant with a fevered imagination revealed a supposed black conspiracy to burn the city, murder white men, and rape white women. Fear and hysteria led to promiscuous accusations against innocent people. Vengeful juries were busy for over a year convicting black men. Eighteen slaves were hanged, 13 were burned at the stake, and more than 150 were imprisoned. Four white men who were allegedly implicated in their conspiracy were also hanged, and 25 were imprisoned. When the sixteen-year-old accuser began to name respectable citizens, her accusations lost credibility and the trials ended. Jurors sworn to do justice rarely had achieved such injustice.

Among the few other significant cases before the era of the American Revolution, one occurred in 1754 in Massachusetts, when Daniel Fowle, a printer, was imprisoned for his libels on the government of Massachusetts. Defending himself by invoking Magna Carta and due process, Fowle angrily complained that he had been denied trial by jury. He was eventually freed and received damages for his losses, a reaffirmation of the sole power of a jury to deny a person's life, liberty, or property.

When judges were dependent tools of the government, a jury of one's peers or neighbors might seem to be a promising bulwark against tyrannous prosecution—though grand juries were also supposed to prevent that possibility. That the jury would protect unpopular defendants was an accepted article of faith. Juries had acquitted William Bradford, Thomas Maule, and Peter Zenger. But if a grand jury indicted or a crown prosecutor proceeded by information, a trial jury, with the power of ruling on guilt or innocence, might be as influenced by prevailing passions as judges when deciding the fate of unpopular defendants. In England, where the power of juries to decide the law as well as the facts in libel cases was secured by Fox's Libel Act of 1792, the most repressive prosecutions, with few exceptions, were successful. In America only one verdict of not guilty was returned in the numerous prosecutions under the Sedition Act of 1798, which also protected the power of juries over the law.

Furthermore, the right to trial by jury could be circumvented by a legislature's power of parliamentary privilege, which came into play whenever a popular assembly believed itself to have been affronted. It could summon the offender before its bar and punish him. Scores of such instances existed, one in 1758 in the Smith-Moore case in Pennsylvania. William Moore, an Anglican who was chief judge of a county court, engaged in a dispute with Quakers on the subject of a defensive war. The Quaker-dominated Assembly summoned him for questioning. His friend William Smith, also an Anglican and president of the college that became the University of Pennsylvania, tried to assist him, thereby earning the anger of the Assembly. That body ordered the arrest of Smith and Moore. They denied the Assembly's authority and demanded their right to trial by jury. But they received only a mock trial before a kangaroo court acting as accuser, judge, and jury. They were convicted despite their claims of innocence. The prisoners petitioned the chief justice of the province's highest court, which ruled that they could not be granted a writ of habeas corpus or even be bailed, because the Assembly had imprisoned them for breach of parliamentary privilege.

In 1760 Richard Bland, a Virginia aristocrat and scholar who served for three decades in the Virginia House of Burgesses, published his influential tract lauding trial by jury as an essential component of the British constitution. A year later in Massachusetts, a jury triumphantly disobeyed a court's instructions, which other judges and the provincial governor supported. The trial court acknowledged that it had no jurisdiction to set aside the jury's verdict even if the verdict violated the court's determination of the law. So too the high court of Connecticut refused to grant a new trial after a jury's verdict challenged the law laid down by the court. The judges declared that the verdict remained valid even if "the jury have mistaken the law or evidence, for by the practice of this state, they are judges of both." What the Connecticut court said might have been endorsed by the courts of all the other colonies. None disagreed. Some, like Georgia, constitutionally prohibited judges from interfering with a jury's determination of the law, and other states, like New Jersey, similarly prohibited judges from doing so by statute. Virginia's court explicitly refused to upset a jury verdict that conflicted with the evidence.

New Yorkers protested when their royal governor, Cadwallader Colden, subverted trial by jury in the Forcey case, which stretched from the fall of 1764 to the close of 1766, alarming all the colonies because of the governor's assault on trial by jury. Forcey was the victim of a physical attack by one Cunningham, who was steeply fined for the offense. But Cunningham expected the New York Supreme Court to grant him relief from the excessive award of civil damages made by a jury, or at least to permit him to appeal to the governor in Council to cancel or modify the jury verdict. The court ruled against Cunningham. Colden, however, ordered the court to allow the Council to review and overturn the proceedings. The court refused on the ground that its compliance with the governor's orders would violate the law of the land and threaten the right to trial by jury. The dispute became notorious. A writer in a New York weekly publication repudiated the "unconstitutional and illegal" assault on trial by jury, and a grand jury, convened to investigate the case, agreed that upsetting the verdict subverted the right to trial by jury. The New York Assembly denounced the governor and reaffirmed trial by jury as the palladium of personal rights.

Jury verdicts punctuated the bizarre story of a Connecticut man who lived with two women, lawfully it seemed. For several years he had been monogamous. Then, sometime in the 1760s, a woman from abroad arrived in town and took up residence with him and the other woman. From the way the three comported themselves, the townsfolk understood that the man was sleeping with both women. Accordingly he was prosecuted for adultery, but when he produced marriage licenses showing that he was wed to each woman, the jury acquitted. The town prosecutor then sought to convict him for the crime of bigamy. Again a jury acquitted, this time because the man showed that under an act of the legislature, if a spouse was missing for more than five years and believed to be dead, the remaining partner might remarry. After juries in effect sanctioned lawful bigamy, the only way to break up the notorious three-way relationship was for one of the women to seek an annulment of her marriage. Yet neither woman would sue for an annulment. Each claimed to have no objection with the *ménage à trois*. They had become good friends, and the older one thought the other was a great help around the house. The husband enjoyed the sexual favors of both women, and nothing could be done about the situation, thanks to the jury verdicts on his behalf.

By the era of the American Revolution, trial by jury was probably the most common right in all the colonies. Americans saw it as a basic guarantor of individual freedom. Edmund Burke, the British statesman, warned Parliament that the colonies would rebel against legislation that deprived them of the benefits of trial by jury. Nevertheless, Parliament imposed the Stamp Act of 1765, authorizing admiralty courts to enforce its provisions. John Adams voiced the American reaction when he wrote: "But the most grievous innovation of all, is the alarming extension of the power of courts of admiralty. In these courts, one judge presides alone! No juries have any concern there! The law and the fact are both to be decided by the same single judge."

The town of Boston notified its representatives in the provincial legislature that "the most essential Rights of British subjects" were representation and trial by jury, calling the latter "the very Ballast of the British Constitution." The Stamp Act Congress protested the denial of trial by jury, which it pronounced to be one of the most essential liberties of the colonists, "the inherent and invaluable right of every British subject." The Massachusetts legislature, in resolves framed by Samuel Adams, asserted that "the extension of the powers of the Court of Admiralty within this province is a most violent infraction of the right of trials by juries—a right which this House, upon the principles of their British ancestors, hold most dear and sacred, it being the only security of the lives, liberties, and properties of his Majesty's subjects here."

Even so, in the Townshend Acts of 1767 Parliament made offenses triable by admiralty courts sitting without juries, with the result that the colonists, vehemently protesting, indulged in statements decrying tyranny and extolling trial by jury. The obnoxious measures were not repealed until 1770. A year before then, John Tabor Kempe, the attorney general of New York who had a first-rate English legal education, made a statement that one might expect from a defense attorney, not a prosecutor. In a letter to three Suffolk County justices, Kempe criticized their enforcement of an act that authorized them to proceed summarily in vagrancy cases. He claimed that their conduct revealed an absence of constitutional scruple. The act's purpose, he noted, was to prevent the imprisonment of disorderly persons from becoming a burden to the county; it "must not be extended beyond that, as it destroys the trial by jury." Replying to a request for instructions, he added: "It may not be improper to presume that the whole scope of that act is of a very extraordinary nature and appears upon very little reflection to be destructive of that Grand Bulwark of our Freedom and Safety, the tryal by Jury, inasmuch as it is calculated to enable magistrates to punish the subject criminally without the judgment of their peers." Today justices of the peace continue to exercise summary powers in petty cases, including vagrancy, dispensing justice without trial by jury.

When juries sat, they controlled justice. In 1771 John Adams confided to his diary that a jury could determine the law no matter how a court instructed it. A juror had to follow his own understanding, Adams believed, even if "in direct opposition to the direction of the court." The Boston town meeting of 1772, which framed "A List of Infringements and Violations of Rights," included trial by jury, which it hailed as "the grand bulwark and security of English property." Selectively quoting from Blackstone's *Commentaries*, the colonists praised his remarks to the effect that trial by jury was the "sacred palladium" of English liberties that might be undermined by new or different methods of trial. Massachusetts lawyers normally argued the law to juries.

Americans formally claimed trial by a jury of the vicinage as a right of Englishmen whenever they apprehended that Britain threatened that right, as when a provision of the Coercive Acts of 1774 authorized trial in England of certain persons who violated the acts in America. William Henry Drayton, an American patriot who served as a royal judge in South Carolina and a member of that colony's privy council, addressed an influential letter to the Continental Congress, which was soon to meet. He framed a constitutional argument on behalf of the American cause, in which he associated trial by jury with Magna Carta. Because of his opinions, he was removed from both the bench and the council. In his defense he protested his denial of the right to trial by jury. His protest was widely circulated as a significant statement on behalf of the rights of Englishmen, rights rapidly becoming American. Moreover, the Continental Congress approved of an intercolonial "Declaration of Rights" based on natural law, the English constitution, and the provincial charters. The Declaration of Rights included "the great and inestimable privilege of being tried by their peers of the vicinage" according to the common law. And when Congress sought to enlist Canadian support for its cause, its letter to the inhabitants of Quebec, in 1774, specified trial by jury as the preserver of life, liberty, and property against arbitrary and capricious men. In the 1775 Declaration of the Causes and Necessity of Taking Up Arms, Congress censured Britain for having enacted statutes "extending the jurisdiction of courts of admiralty and vice-admiralty beyond their ancient limits, for depriving us of the accustomed and inestimable privilege of trial by jury, in cases affecting both life and property." In the

Declaration of Independence, Congress criticized George III for "depriving us, in many cases, of the benefit of trial by jury."

When Virginia framed its constitution in 1776, the first state to do so, it declared that in all criminal prosecutions the defendant had a right to a "speedy trial by an impartial jury of his vicinage," language echoed by Pennsylvania. Notwithstanding that provision in Virginia's constitution, the state in 1778 enacted a bill of attainder and outlawry drafted by Thomas Jefferson at the instigation of Governor Patrick Henry, against a reputed cutthroat Tory, one Josiah Philips, and some fifty unnamed "associates." By legislative enactment they were condemned, without trial, for treason and murder, and on failure to surrender were subject to being killed on sight by anyone.

At the Virginia ratifying convention in 1788, Edmund Randolph, irked beyond endurance by Patrick Henry's assaults on the Constitution as dangerous to personal liberties, recalled with "horror," he said, the "shocking" attainder, which was a legislative act pronouncing the guilt of a person without affording him a trial by jury. When Henry defended the attainder, John Marshall, who would become the nation's greatest chief justice and who supported ratification, declared, "Without a bill of rights can we pretend to the enjoyment of political freedom or security when we are told that a man has been, by an act of the Assembly, struck out of existence without a trial by jury, without examination, without being confronted by his accusers and witnesses, without the benefits of the law of the land?" In fact, however, Philips did receive a trial.

Delaware's constitution of 1776 described juries as the triers of fact and added that no person accused of crime should be found guilty unless he had received a speedy trial by an impartial jury. Maryland copied Delaware's language. North Carolina's language was similar to that of Virginia, which, as previously indicated, ensured the criminally accused a speedy trial by a jury of the vicinage. Vermont also guaranteed a speedy trial by "an impartial jury of the country," and Georgia by its constitution of 1777 provided that "the jury shall be judges of law, as well as fact." A Connecticut court in 1788 repudiated the claim that a jury's judgment should be overturned because the jury had gotten the law wrong in a case. The court ruled that "it doth not vitiate a verdict, that the jury have mistaken the law or the evidence; for by the practice of this state, they are judges of both." Massachusetts framed a provision that influenced the writing of the United States Bill of Rights, saying that the legislature should not subject any person to capital or infamous punishment without trial by jury. New Hampshire adopted the identical language. No other personal right excepting religious liberty received protection from the constitutions of so many states.

Thomas Jefferson, in his *Notes on Virginia*, published in 1783, endorsed the jury's broad power over the law. "It is usual for the jurors to decide the fact," he wrote, "and to refer the law arising on it to the decision of judges. But this division of the subject lies with their [the jury's] discretion only. And if the question relates to any point of public liberty, or if it be one of those in which the judge may be suspected of bias, the jury undertake to decide both the law and fact." Jefferson, in effect, reported an existing situation.

In the 1786 case of *Trevett v. Weeden* in Rhode Island, at issue was a state act that compelled the observance of a paper-money measure that made anyone refusing to accept paper money at par with specie triable without a jury. The act was an exceptionable betrayal of previously professed commitments to trial by jury. The Northwest Ordinance of 1787, that measure of genius which thwarted the development of colonial problems on the American continent by guaranteeing statehood to territories, ensured trial by jury. In *Bayard v. Singleton*, decided in North Carolina in 1787, the high court of that state supported trial by jury against a legislative attempt to undermine it in a case involving property rights. The legislature summoned the judges before it to determine whether they had committed malpractice by refusing to give effect to the statute that subverted trial by jury. The court defiantly held void the measure that adversely affected the right to trial by jury on behalf of one of the parties. The court then submitted the case to a jury, and the legislature, despite threats, eventually backed down.

At the Philadelphia Constitutional Convention of 1787, the first right recognized was trial by jury. The convention did not frame a bill of rights but included several rights within the body of the Constitution. The New Jersey Plan of Union had proposed "that no person shall be liable to be tried for any criminal offense, committed within any of the United States, in any other state than that wherein the offense shall be committed, nor be deprived of the privilege of trial by jury, by virtue of any law of the United States." The Committee on Detail adopted the gist of that proposal. A recommendation of

John Rutledge of South Carolina provided for trial by jury in criminal cases in the state that was the locale of the offense. James Wilson of Pennsylvania and Charles Pinckney of South Carolina lent their support to such a provision. It eventually became lodged in Article III, section 2 of the Constitution, which said in part: "The trial of all crimes, except in cases of impeachment, shall be by jury; and such trial shall be held in the state where the said crimes shall have been committed; but when not committed within any state, the trial shall be at such place or places as the Congress may by law have directed."

The right to trial by jury in civil cases received belated recognition when Elbridge Gerry of Massachusetts claimed that civil juries guarded against corrupt judges. Pinckney cooperated with Gerry in urging a provision that would secure trial by jury "as usual in civil cases," but the convention let the recommendation die when others observed that jury practices throughout the nation were not uniform, so no one could be sure of the meaning of the phrase "as usual." Gerry, who refused to sign the Constitution, inaccurately declared that it established a "tribunal without juries, which will be a Star-chamber as to Civil cases." George Mason of Virginia, who belatedly lamented the omission of a bill of rights, offered a few specific recommendations, including trial by jury in civil cases.

During the controversy over the ratification of the Constitution, trial by jury received extreme acclamations. An anonymous Anti-Federalist described it as "the first privilege of freemen—the noblest article that ever entered the constitution of a free country—a jewel whose transcendent lustre adds dignity to human nature." The Constitution's omission of trial by jury in civil cases gave the Anti-Federalists an opportunity to denigrate the Constitution and to extol trial by jury as a "sacred" right without which tyranny would ensue. This was one of the most frequently trumpeted Anti-Federalist claims.

Richard Henry Lee of Virginia was one of the first of several Anti-Federalists to declare misleadingly that the Constitution, if ratified, would abolish trial by jury in civil cases. He invoked the great English legal luminaries—Coke, Hale, Holt, and Blackstone—and, he claimed, "almost every other legal or political scholar" to prove that trial by jury in civil cases was necessary to maintain freedom and to keep courts from becoming arbitrary. "Would any man oppose government," he added, "where his property would be wholly at the mercy and decision of those that govern? . . . And a government, where there is no trial by jury, has an unlimited command over every man who has any thing to lose. It is by the attacks on private property through the judiciary that despotism becomes as irresistible as terrible." Patrick Henry also promiscuously alleged that the Constitution jeopardized trial by jury.

The influential minority report of the Anti-Federalists of Pennsylvania declared, misleadingly, that trial by jury in civil cases ought not to be abolished—as if it had been. Judge George Bryan of Pennsylvania, a prolific essayist writing as "Centinel," predicted in a Philadelphia newspaper that the federal courts would "supersede the state courts" because of the Constitution's failure to provide for civil jury trials. Bryan insisted that only the jury could preserve for the people their share in the administration justice and prevent "the encroachments of the more powerful and wealthy citizens." Oligarchs, he wrote, would be uncontrolled but for juries.

Whenever juries had been abolished, asserted "An Old Whig," the liberties of the people were quickly lost. He repudiated the Federalist assertion that criminal juries were sufficient to guard against tyranny and asserted: "Are there not a thousand civil cases in which the government is a party? In all the actions for penalties, forfeitures and public debts, as well as many others, the government is a party and the whole weight of the government is thrown into the scale of the prosecution, yet these are all of them civil causes. . . . These modes of harassing the subject have perhaps been more effectual than direct criminal prosecutions."

Another Anti-Federalist, Abiel Holmes of Plymouth County, Massachusetts, objected in the Massachusetts ratifying convention that the Constitution did not properly provide for trial by jury because it did not vest a right to demand a trial where an offense occurred and where a jury would, "from the local situation, have an opportunity to form a judgment of the character of the person charged with the crime, and also to judge of the credibility of the witnesses." The Constitution provided for a jury trial, Holmes remarked, but did not indicate "who this jury is to be, how qualified, where to live, how appointed, or by what rules to regulate their procedure." Christopher Gore of Boston responded that jurors no longer needed to know the neighborhood where the crime occurred and that the diversity of practice in the states explained why the Constitution could not have been more specific about the matter.

The minority in Maryland, with restraint and good sense, urged a protection that "there shall be a trial by jury in all criminal cases according to the course of proceeding in the state where the offence is committed." Oddly, the same source said nothing of jury trials in civil cases, but at least the Maryland minority did not distort the Constitution's provision for trial by jury, as most other Anti-Federalists did. "Aristocrotis," the author of a pamphlet published in Pennsylvania, sarcastically distorted facts. Predicting that Congress would deprive the people of trial by jury, because it was so absurd a right, he claimed that it allowed twelve ignorant and probably illiterate plebeians to be judges of the law as if they had the authority of lawyers sitting in legislatures and courts. With no sarcasm whatever, "Columbian Patriot," who was probably Mercy Otis Warren, writing in a Boston newspaper, insinuated that an "inquisition" would be the result of the abolition of trial by jury in civil cases. Seven states recommended an amendment to the Constitution insuring the right. Everyone, Federalists included, believed in trial by jury in civil cases at the very least because jury verdicts were more reliable than bench verdicts.

George Washington reported to Lafayette that although all members of the Constitutional Convention believed in "Tryal by Jury," they left to future consideration a decision on how to provide for it without interfering "with the fixed modes of any of the States." Alexander Hamilton believed that the "objection to the plan of the convention, which has met with the most success," in New York "and perhaps in several of the other States, is that relative to the want of a constitutional provision for the trial by jury in civil cases"—an omission, he noted, that was inadvertent. Hamilton published the fullest and best refutation of Anti-Federalist hysteria on the issue in his long essay in *Federalist* No. 83, in which he discoursed on the differences in state practices and on the power of Congress to establish courts and therefore trial by jury. He denied that the provision for it in criminal cases implied that its omission in civil cases was in effect a prohibition. As "a valuable safeguard to liberty" and "the very palladium of free government," everyone respected trial by jury, though Hamilton confessed himself unable to discern its inseparable connection to liberty in civil cases. Its value, rather, consisted in its security against corruption. Sheriffs and clerks of courts who chose juries were most likely to be corrupted, less so judges and still less so jurors.

But, Hamilton thought, the differences among the states concerning trial by jury militated against prescribing one form for all states. Connecticut, he noted, tried admiralty cases with a jury, New York did not. Equity cases, prize cases, and others involving international law also posed obstacles to the imposition of a uniform jury system. Failure to provide constitutional protection in civil cases did not bar its later provision by Congress after proper consideration of the problems that the convention had not considered. James Wilson of Pennsylvania, second only to Madison as a framer with exceptional influence, agreed with Hamilton and argued too that a provision for a uniform system of trial by jury might conflict with state provisions, which varied considerably. That was an odd argument, because a uniform system of trial by jury in the federal courts had nothing to do with the various state provisions.

The cool analysis of a Hamilton or Wilson did not quell Anti-Federalist suspicions of the proposed national government respecting the jury issue. Some of the Anti-Federalist hysteria regarding trial by jury may be explained as a reaction to its attempted subversion in several states by state authorities in whom the Anti-Federalists reposed their trust. In a Pennsylvania case of 1784, *Respublica v. Doan*, the defendant was legislatively convicted for a felony and outlawed. When he was captured, the state ordered his execution, but he demanded a trial by jury, which was guaranteed by the state constitution. The state judges, however, ruled that Doan had in effect rejected trial by jury when he fled from custody and became a fugitive. He was hanged without having had a trial by jury.

The scandal of the Doan case outraged people throughout the country and strengthened the demands that jury trials should be ensured. "Democratic Federalist," a Pennsylvania writer opposed to ratification, argued that the Constitution "entirely and effectually abolished" trial by jury in civil cases. He claimed that the new national courts could not possibly travel around the whole country and conduct trials with verdicts given by juries of the vicinage. Similarly, "Cincinnatus" warned that if a new Zenger case arose involving freedom of the press, the Constitution "was so admirably framed for tyranny, that, by clear construction, the judges might put the verdict of a jury out of the question." He predicted that without trial by jury, a new Star Chamber would arise. Only the jury, he contended, had saved Zenger. He did not notice that Zenger had been prosecuted criminally, not civilly, when he argued that a jury alone could save a future printer "from the fangs of power," nor did he notice that the Constitution guaranteed jury trial in cases of crimes.

The Pennsylvania minority did take notice of the fact but contended that the omission of jury trials in civil cases portended despotism and aristocratic rule; moreover, even in cases of crimes, the common people would be deprived of trial by a jury of the vicinage. Luther Martin of Maryland, expanding this notion, bemoaned the need of a defendant "to travel perhaps more than a thousand miles" in a case involving violation of national law. Other Anti-Federalists claimed that the American Revolution had been fought for trial by jury. As one wrote, with extraordinary oversimplification, "What made the people revolt from Great Britain? The trial by jury, that great safeguard of liberty, was taken away."

Similarly, Richard Henry Lee, writing as "Federal Farmer," added that proceedings in the new national courts would be "secret and arbitrary," making indispensable trial by jury in civil as well as criminal cases, because jurors could not be corrupted; their identities would be unknown until the hour of a trial. Without juries to check "the arbitrary power of judges," judges would become "increasingly despotic or corrupt." Without juries, "the liberties of the people were soon lost." Without juries, the government had an unlimited command over every person with anything to lose. Juries were democratic, the people's agency. Said Lee:

> The jury trial, especially politically considered, is by far the most important feature in the judicial department of a

free country. . . . Juries are constantly and frequently drawn from the body of the people, and freemen of the country; and by holding the jury's right to return a general verdict in all cases sacred, we secure to the people at large, their just and rightful controul in the judicial department. . . . The body of the people, principally, bear the burdens of the community; they of right ought to have a controul in its important concerns, both in making [by legislation] and executing [through juries] the laws, otherwise they may, in a short time, be ruined.

In the Massachusetts ratifying convention, one Anti-Federalist delegate even charged that national officers might file informations against innocent persons, drag them from homes and families, and imprison them—all without trial. "Are there not a thousand civil cases in which the government is a party?" asked another Anti-Federalist. The government was a "party in all actions for penalties, forfeitures, and public debts," he asserted, and all were civil cases. Still another Anti-Federalist expressed the fear that if judges were unchecked by juries, the people would be judicially coerced into submission to the government. Even if they had a trial, he added, the Constitution said nothing about who their juries would be, how qualified they would be, how they would be appointed, and what rules would regulate their procedures. As a result, Congress could institute the Spanish Inquisition. Again and again Anti-Federalists selectively quoted from Blackstone to support the contention that without civil jury trials the more powerful and wealthy citizens would control the administration of justice and freely encroach on the common people. Juries were bulwarks against private as well as public oppression. The only agency of government that powerful and wealthy "oligarchs" could not control was a jury. Seven states urged an amendment to the Constitution guaranteeing trial by jury in civil cases.

At about the same time, 1788, a Connecticut court reconfirmed a jury's authority. The case involved a suit by a black slave for his freedom. His alleged owner challenged a juror for believing that a Negro, by the laws of Connecticut, could not be held in slavery. The highest court of the state sustained the trial judge's ruling that an "opinion formed and declared upon a general principle of law, does not disqualify a juror to sit in a cause in which that principle applies." In another case the state's highest court said flat out that a verdict was not invalid despite a jury's having "mistaken the law or the evidence, for by the practice of this state, they are judges of both." Every New England state followed the same practice. Indeed, a different practice cannot be found anywhere else in the nation.

In 1791 Robert Coram of Wilmington, Delaware, the editor of the *Delaware Gazette* and an Anti-Federalist, published a little book entitled *Political Inquiries*. He asserted that trial by jury depended on the "natural intellectual equality" predominate in free countries. "Otherwise would they have suffered the unlettered peasant to decide against lawyers and judges?" The peasant's common sense enabled him to distinguish right from wrong so that he could overcome his ignorance of legal technicalities.

In the First Congress, Representative James Madison recommended amendments to the Constitution that became the

Bill of Rights. One of his proposals, which he conceived to be "the most valuable amendment in the whole list," would have prohibited the states from infringing on various rights, including trial by jury in criminal cases. Madison's proposal was that the "trial of all crimes . . . shall be by an impartial jury of freeholders of the vicinage." The proposal related to crimes against national law, and it excepted crimes in any county that might be in enemy possession or in which an insurrection was occurring.

Madison's proposals were reviewed by a select committee consisting of one delegate from each of the eleven states that by then had ratified the Constitution. The House of Representatives altered the jury proposal by providing that trials should be by "juries of the vicinage." The Senate, controlled by Federalists, was not keen on that. Madison observed that the senators were "inflexible in opposing a definition of the locality of the juries. The vicinage they contend is either too vague or too strict a term, too vague if depending on limits to be fixed by the pleasure of the law, too strict if limited to the County." What he meant was that "the vicinage" lacked a legal meaning and could mean different things in different states. He also was concerned that local juries might protect local rebels from national prosecution. Accordingly the Senate voted to delete the language of the House concerning the vicinage.

The Senate preferred the national government to have the authority to select a trial location and a jury from any place within a state where a crime occurred. Restricting trials to the county where a crime occurred was too rigid. The House, seeking a compromise, proposed: "In all criminal prosecutions, the accused shall enjoy the right to speedy and public trial, by an impartial jury of the state and district where in the crime shall have been committed, which district shall have been previously ascertained by law." That compromise prevailed and also became part of the language of the Judiciary Act of 1789, which established eleven judicial districts, one for each state; the districts pretty much followed state boundaries. The act also provided that in cases punishable by death, "the trial shall be held in the County where the offence was committed, or where that cannot be done without inconvenience, Twelve petit Jurors at least, shall be summoned thence." That preserved the convention that jurors should come from the vicinage and that trials should be held in that locality.

In the same year the Bill of Rights was ratified, 1791, James Wilson of Pennsylvania endorsed the right of juries to decide legal issues as well as factual ones. Although a court had a right to instruct a jury on the law of a case, he said in his famous law lectures, the jury could in effect overrule the court.

The Supreme Court of the United States also endorsed the power of juries. In *Georgia v. Brailsford*, decided in 1794, Chief Justice John Jay reminded a jury of "the good old rule, that on questions of fact, it is the province of the jury, on questions of law, it is the province of the court to decide. But it must be observed that by the same law, which recognizes the reasonable distribution of jurisdiction, you have nevertheless the right to take upon yourselves to judge of both, and to determine the law as well as the fact in controversy." Both, Jay added, were lawfully within the jury's power of decision. In 1795 Zephaniah Swift, in his book on the law of Connecticut, declared that the "jury were the proper judges, not only of the fact but of the law that was necessarily involved" in each case and that the jury had "a right to do as they please" without their verdicts being rejected.

Three years later, when Congress debated the infamous Sedition Act, the role of the jury in prosecutions had a prominent part. In the course of muzzling freedom of speech and press, the House made certain that trial by jury was the means of determining the guilt of accused persons. William Claiborne of Tennessee moved that in all cases arising under the Sedition Act, "the jury who shall try the cause, shall be judges of the law as well as the fact." He wished to be sure, he said, that no judicial officer would decide what utterances were libelous. Nathaniel Smith of Connecticut, replying that such a provision was unnecessary, alleged that the motion would vest juries with the power to judge law as well as fact, thereby making the jury superior to a court when determining the legality of testimony. James Bayard of Delaware, agreeing with Smith, claimed that the motion would empower juries, rather than judges, to determine a matter of constitutionality. Albert Gallatin proposed a compromise drawn from the constitution of his own state of Pennsylvania, allowing juries to have "the same power to decide on the criminality of the act, which they had in other cases." His proposal, which was adopted and became part of the Sedition Act, was that "the jury should have the right to determine the law and the fact, under the direction of the court, as in other cases."

That became the American standard, which was confirmed when the administration of President Thomas Jefferson prosecuted Harry Croswell, the editor of a Federalist publication, *The Wasp*, for the supposed crime of libeling Jefferson. In 1803 Croswell was convicted in a trial court of New York presided over by the Jeffersonian chief justice, Morgan Lewis. Lewis actually refused a request that Croswell be allowed to prove the truth of his charges against Jefferson. He instructed the jury that truth was not a defense against a charge of seditious libel and that the jury's only duty was to find whether the defendant had in fact published the statement charged, leaving to the court the decision whether the publication was criminal as a matter of law. Lewis would have turned the law back to the pre-Zenger era, as would the jury that convicted Lewis.

On appeal, Alexander Hamilton represented Croswell before the full bench of the state's high court. Hamilton argued that the jury should decide the criminality of the publication and that it should acquit if it found that the publication was true and had been published with good motives for justifiable ends. The opinion of Judge James Kent, which came to be the American standard, restated Hamilton's argument. Kent, believing that the mere act of publication could not in itself be criminal, emphasized that criminality consisted "in a malicious and seditious intention," whose existence a jury must determine in any criminal case. To deny the jury the right of deciding the intent and tendency of the publication deprived the defendant of the substance and security of a jury trial. Moreover, Kent concluded, unless the jury considered the truth of the defendant's statements, it could not determine his motive in making them and thereby abridged the means of defense.

As a result of this case, the New York legislature enacted a bill in 1805 allowing the jury to decide the criminality of an alleged libel and permitting truth as a defense if published with good motives for justifiable ends. That standard slowly spread throughout the nation as the proper one. Thus trial by jury, a right fictively derived from Magna Carta, became the Anglo-American palladium of justice.

A NOTE ON SOURCES

J. S. COCKBURN and Thomas A. Green have edited *Twelve Good Men and True: The Criminal Trial Jury in England, 1200–1800* (Princeton, 1985), an outstanding collection of essays by specialists who focus narrowly on particular aspects of the subject, such as the Hertford juries of 1573–1624 and the Devon juries of 1649–1670. James Bradley Thayer's *Preliminary Treatise of Evidence at Common Law* (Boston, 1896), a great legal historian's masterwork, is more than a century old but still indispensable for its few chapters, however dense, on trial by jury. Lysander Spooner's *An Essay on the Trial by Jury*, a pioneering work of 1852, is based on the mistaken belief that Magna Carta established trial by jury. Jeffrey Abramson, *We the Jury: The Jury System and the Ideal of Democracy* (New York, 1994), an outstanding book, is a splendid defense of jury trials, countering critics, by a lawyer and political scientist especially interested in jury selection and the death penalty.

Richard D. Younger, *The People's Panel: The Grand Jury in the United States, 1634–1941* (Providence, R.I., 1963) is the best review of the history of the grand jury but has far too little on the subject before 1800. Francis H. Heller, *The Sixth Amendment to the Constitution of the United States* (Lawrence, Kans., 1951) is a useful and comprehensive treatment of all aspects of the subject, including speedy trial and juries of the vicinage. Samuel W. McCart, *Trial by Jury: A Complete Guide to the Jury System* (Philadelphia, 1964) is broad yet superficial and unhistorical.

In 1950 Majorie Schultz edited *The American Jury* for *Law and Contemporary Problems*, an anthology in which experts write specialized essays without historical value. Harry Kalven and Hans Zeisel, two academic lawyers, wrote the massive, fascinating, and highly controversial book *The American Jury* (Boston, 1966), revealing what they overheard when eavesdropping on a jury's deliberations. Lawrence M. Friedman's *Crime and Punishment in American History* (New York, 1993) is a superb general history of criminal justice that too briefly treats trial by jury. Charles H. Whitebread's *Criminal Procedure* (Westbury, N.Y., 1980) is a legal treatise, intended for law students, which offers an analysis of modern Supreme Court decisions; one chapter covers jury trials, and another speedy trials.

INDEX

A NOTE ON THE AUTHOR

Leonard W. Levy, whose *Origins of the Fifth Amendment* was awarded the Pulitzer Prize in history, is formerly Earl Warren Professor of Constitutional History at Brandeis University and Andrew W. Mellon All-Claremont Professor of Humanities and History at the Claremont Graduate School. His other writings, many of which have also won awards, include *Blasphemy, The Establishment Clause, Freedom of the Press from Zenger to Jefferson, Legacy of Suppression*, and *Jefferson and Civil Liberties*. Mr. Levy lives in Ashland, Oregon.